A NEW
SCIENCE
OF THE
AFTERLIFE

"In his mind-bending book, Dan Drasin draws on his more than three decades of investigation into the areas of consciousness research and paranormal experiences to arrive at a new and compelling vision of what actually awaits us when we die. By dismantling the structures of an outworn materialistic worldview, Drasin reveals that the afterlife constitutes a legitimate arena of scientific research and that it can be objectively demonstrated. This groundbreaking book provides solid grounds for believing that death is anything but a dead end."

KENNETH RING, PH.D., AUTHOR OF *LESSONS FROM THE LIGHT*

"A New Science of the Afterlife is a uniquely inspiring fusion of clarity, accessibility, wit, and insight. It is a precious gift for the curious newcomer, the spiritual seeker, and the resolute scientist seeking to engage with the growing body of evidence for a 'greater reality.' This book is an outstanding contribution to the blossoming field of consciousness studies."

LESLIE KEAN, INVESTIGATIVE JOURNALIST AND
AUTHOR OF *SURVIVING DEATH*

"To mainstream science the survival of consciousness after bodily death is regarded only as a comforting fantasy. But as science marches on, our understanding of reality also changes. As new worldviews arise the possibility of an afterlife takes on a whole new life. This is the exciting story of *A New Science of the Afterlife.*"

DEAN RADIN, PH.D., CHIEF SCIENTIST AT THE INSTITUTE OF
NOETIC SCIENCES AND AUTHOR OF *REAL MAGIC*

"An extremely important book. Drasin's calm, insightful, and brilliant exploration of the subject reveals how science has begun to reintroduce an awareness of spirit and soul into modern intellectual culture. It is deeply heartening, even thrilling, in the convincing, careful way it illuminates multiple perspectives on extra-physical life and reveals what it is like to experience it. One of the great afterlife books of the era."

WHITLEY STRIEBER, AUTHOR OF *COMMUNION* AND
COAUTHOR OF *THE AFTERLIFE REVOLUTION*

"Daniel Drasin is an explorer in a very new way of looking at the survival of consciousness. Daniel tackles not only the 'next life' but also consciousness itself and how it functions—maybe even what it is."

P. M. H. ATWATER, L.H.D., RESEARCHER OF
NEAR-DEATH STATES AND AUTHOR OF
THE NEW CHILDREN AND NEAR-DEATH EXPERIENCES

A NEW SCIENCE
OF THE
AFTERLIFE

Space, Time, and
the Consciousness Code

A Sacred Planet Book

DANIEL DRASIN

Park Street Press
Rochester, Vermont

Park Street Press
One Park Street
Rochester, Vermont 05767
www.ParkStPress.com

Park Street Press is a division of Inner Traditions International

Sacred Planet Books are curated by Richard Grossinger, Inner Traditions editorial board member and cofounder and former publisher of North Atlantic Books. The Sacred Planet collection, published under the umbrella of the Inner Traditions family of imprints, includes works on the themes of consciousness, cosmology, alternative medicine, dreams, climate, permaculture, alchemy, shamanic studies, oracles, astrology, crystals, hyperobjects, locutions, and subtle bodies.

Cataloging-in-Publication Data for this title is available from the Library of Congress

ISBN 978-1-64411-681-4 (print)
ISBN 978-1-64411-682-1 (ebook)

Printed and bound in the United States by Versa Press, Inc.

10 9 8 7 6 5 4 3 2 1

Text design and layout by Kenleigh Manseau
This book was typeset in Garamond Premier Pro with Minion Pro and Museo Sans used as display fonts.

To send correspondence to the author of this book, mail a first-class letter to the author c/o Inner Traditions • Bear & Company, One Park Street, Rochester, VT 05767, and we will forward the communication, or contact the author directly at **dandrasin.com.**

I dedicate this book to my late father, Eliazar Lee Drasin, a kindly soul who taught me to be curious, resourceful, scientific, and open-minded.

Acknowledgments

This book is the culmination of over thirty years of curiosity, wonder, and inquiry. Over these three decades I've enjoyed the company—and have benefited from the rich contributions—of innumerable friends, colleagues, scientists, philosophers, artists, authors, and others on both sides of what we call the "veil." I thank them from the bottom of my heart for their support, courage, inspiration, intelligence, and steadfastness, often in the face of formidable social and institutional odds. They include but are by no means limited to: Shoshana Alexander, Joyce Anastasia, Julia Assante, Richard Bach, Martine Baumal, Julie Beischel, Tania Berg, Jamie Butler, Tom and Lisa Butler, Anabela Cardoso, Sam Case, Tim Coleman, Terri Daniel, David Fontana, Neil Freer, Cheryl Ann Fulton, Lori Grace, Lewis Griggs, Richard Grossinger, Tamara Gurbis, Brian Josephson, Leslie Kean, John Keel, Jane Kimbrough, Jon Klimo, Joanie Lippman, Jeanne Love, Mark Macy, Matthew and Jordan McKay, Jeffrey Mishlove, Robert Monroe, Regina Ochoa, Brian O'Leary, David Pursglove, Dean Radin, Kenneth Ring, Ellie Schamber, Stephan Schwartz, The Scole Group, Rupert Sheldrake, Cynthia Spring, Anne and Whitley Strieber, Nancy Talbott, Vicki Talbott, Charles Tart, Jennifer Tayloe, Jacques Vallée, Frances Vaughan, and Marjorie Wolfe.

A very special *thank you!* also goes out to Kayla Toher, my fabulous editor, and to the outstanding team at Inner Traditions.

Contents

PART III
The Nature of the Afterlife

※

Introduction
Why Now?

If you are curious about the possibility of an afterlife but believe that science rules it out, this book may provide some food for thought, some helpful guidance, and perhaps a few surprises. I've written it partly to provide a welcoming space and safe haven for those who, for social or professional reasons, may be reluctant to reveal their interest in such things.

I confess that I've long resisted writing this book. Writing is a tough grind, and my attention span has never won any major awards. (As many a prominent writer has put it, "I hate writing, but I love having written!") I've also spent most of my professional life behind a camera, so this book is a sort of coming-out party for me.

But why now? What has pushed me over the edge?

To begin with, writing this book has been an opportunity to explore my own long-standing passion for this subject matter and to dig deeply into my own motivation for wanting to share it. I've found researching and exploring the evidence for an afterlife to be fascinating, challenging, mind-stretching, and illuminating in its own right. This pilgrimage has covered a lot of territory and led me to a deeper understanding and appreciation of my own life and the lives of others.

Having recently celebrated my eightieth birthday, I feel it's timely to share what I believe I've learned about the journey we'll all sooner or later make to the other side. If this book illuminates or eases that transition for even one reader, or if a handful of readers can say "Hey,

I never thought about it that way!" I feel it will have been well worth the effort.

Finally, considering the state of our world, it seems especially timely to reexamine our culture's dark-and-spooky view of death. Does it perhaps underlie a fear-based view of life that can distort our self-awareness, relationships, ethics, economics, and politics?

Have we overbuilt a civilization to protect ourselves from a fearful superstition of our own making and, in doing so, brought about more of what we've feared most? If so, could a fresh view of what we call "death" transform our view of life for the better? Could it help us avoid, mitigate, or even reverse the kinds of systemic breakdowns that are already causing widespread species extinction and threatening the foundations of our civilization? If such breakdowns continue despite all efforts to forestall them, could it lead us to a more balanced and peaceful acceptance of the inevitable?

So What Are We Talking About Here?

What is death, anyway? Is it like the archaic notion of sailing off the edge of a two-dimensional, flat Earth into oblivion? Or is there an unacknowledged dimension in which we can travel safely over the horizon into a new world? Can we discover that new world for ourselves by bringing curiosity, courage, and scientific integrity to the task?

> *That, I believe, is true science: to follow the data wherever they lead.*
>
> JACQUES VALLÉE, COMPUTER SCIENTIST,
> AUTHOR, AND PIONEERING ANOMALIES RESEARCHER

As both an intellectual and experiential explorer, I've spent the past three decades investigating the possibility that many of our culture's beliefs and assumptions about life, death, and reality may be as archaic and misguided as those prescientific notions that the Earth was flat and at the center of the universe.

Before the year 1500, the Western world took it for granted that our Earth was indeed poised at the center of things and that the Sun and planets all revolved around us. After all, what could have been more obvious? But there were a few little problems with this assumption. For one thing, the motions of the planets made little sense: sometimes they stopped in their tracks, turned around, and moved backward!* How could this be?

Then along came Copernicus and Galileo, who, against formidable social and institutional odds, offered us a simple shift of perspective: Earth and the planets in fact revolve around the Sun! Who'd'a thunk it? Now many baffling things, including those bizarre planetary motions, fell elegantly into place and actually made sense! (Never mind that the Church Fathers of Galileo's time famously refused to look through his telescope. The cat was out of the bag!)

Today we face a similar predicament, in which a broad spectrum of human experiences and robustly documented phenomena seem to make no sense in light of our currently dominant theories and beliefs. But rather than "looking through the telescope"—bringing our curiosity and our best investigative tools and talents to bear—the overwhelming response of our most influential social, scientific, and academic institutions has been to resist and deny these reports. As a result, many who attest to them in good faith are ridiculed, ostracized, or punished, as if we still lived in a dark age determined to defend itself, at all costs, against an encroaching enlightenment. (I, myself, am no stranger to this sort of harsh judgment and carefully avoid discussing such matters with certain personal friends and professional colleagues.)

Let's recall that the Copernican Shift of the Renaissance demanded little more of us than to step back and take a better mental snapshot of our celestial home, now that we knew where to stand and what to look for.

---

*Before Copernicus, predicting planetary motions was a complex, convoluted process. Google "Ptolemaic astronomy."

A good photograph is knowing where to stand.

ANSEL ADAMS,
LEGENDARY PHOTOGRAPHER

So could an equally simple shift of perspective today open up refreshingly new vistas of who we are, what we're doing here, and what happens when we inevitably pass from this embodied life? I firmly believe such a readjustment is possible, at least for those who can embrace it with curiosity, courage, keen intuition, and clear, open minds.

Many of us are being called to this new vision by myriad influences: by the works of courageous writers, scientists, philosophers, and doctors; by those who have been resuscitated from clinical death; and by psychically talented individuals and electronic experimenters apparently in touch with those who have gone before us across the threshold. For some it's the result of undeniable personal experiences or compelling scientific curiosity. For others it's simply a powerful inner calling that cannot be silenced.

To what, exactly, are we being called? Simply to consider the possibility that what we take to be the whole of reality is embedded in a more comprehensive matrix. Some have described this as a "Greater Reality," in which an afterlife exists as obviously and naturally as our physical life exists in our familiar physical universe. Its substance, however, is not said to lie in physicality as we know it but in the seemingly ephemeral realm of *consciousness*.

So what is this thing we're calling "consciousness"? From this unfolding perspective it appears to be an irreducible field of *something* that possesses remarkable properties, notably the capacity for experience, volition, and purpose. Perhaps we need a new word for it, because it seems to be a deeper, broader, richer *something* than what we normally think of as consciousness, just as our spherical Earth is quite different from the flat one that was naively imagined by our dimensionally challenged ancestors.

So Who Am I to Consider Such a Radical View of Reality, Life, and Death?

For most of my adult life I've been a documentary filmmaker and media producer. I've traveled widely, have had a lifelong engagement with the sciences and the arts, and enjoy considering new, unfamiliar, cross-cultural, and interdisciplinary perspectives. As a generalist I feel I have a good vantage point for seeing big-picture connections among things that narrowly focused specialists, for all of their priceless gifts, can sometimes tend to overlook.

Thanks to some interesting experiences I've been blessed with throughout my life, I've long suspected that reality as currently interpreted by our senses, sciences, and society isn't the whole picture. This came into better focus as I began to connect with others who had had similar experiences and suspicions. Virtually all were sane, productive individuals who didn't seem at all misguided, weak-minded, credulous, or superstitious. Some were brilliant visionaries. Some were teachers, doctors, journalists, and businessfolk. Some were working scientists.

What were we seeing and suspecting in common? Simply that the familiar physical universe we take to be the whole of reality may in fact be only the tip of an iceberg—the visible surface of a deeper, richer, more colorful realm that's made of different stuff and plays by a more lively and creative set of rules.

This "Greater Reality" is said to be where our awareness—in other words, our self, soul, being or essence—resides between and beyond our space-and-time-bound physical lives. Though this reality may be heavily masked by our powerful physical senses and habits of mind, we may get tantalizing glimpses of it when our awareness is dilated or redirected during lucid dreams, meditation, sensory-deprivation sessions, psychedelic journeys, near-death experiences, or quiet moments under the night sky.

The main purpose of this book is to explore how we might better recognize, demystify, appreciate, and befriend that Greater Reality while still living fruitfully in the physical world.

Where Am I Coming From?

While I am not a credentialed scientist, I will be quoting and paraphrasing more than a few accomplished scientists, artists, philosophers, and academics. My goal is not to create yet another chapter-and-verse belief system; it is simply to present for your consideration a vision of reality that goes hand in glove with some astonishing recent discoveries by several emerging branches of science. If these insights are on the mark, perhaps this new vision might help us turn the right corner at a critical juncture in our evolving journey on this planet and beyond.

Where Do _You_ Come From?

In our views of the afterlife or anything else, each of us comes from our own unique vantage point based on our personal store of experience, knowledge, attitudes, education, and conditioning. So some things may be more visible or thinkable to some of us than to others. Some may use different language to describe the same things, or the same language to describe different things. We'll do our best with this and seek out metaphors to bridge our varied language and experiences and perhaps to open minds to possibilities not yet considered.

A Few Final Notes

Theories and abstractions have their place, but they don't dictate reality. So in this book we'll be focusing mainly on concrete observations, robust evidence, and some exercises we can play with to expand and hone our perceptions. As we shall see, some things we might assume to be improbable or even unthinkable may turn out to be surprisingly familiar once we notice them already at play in our everyday lives.

Here are a few more things to keep in mind as we prepare to survey this new territory together.

- In exploring outside the box of common consensus I think it's essential that we become aware of our beliefs and be willing to suspend them for a time. This does not mean abandoning them, but it does mean setting them aside long enough to nibble at other possibilities and roll them around on our mind's tongue. We don't want to swallow them unless they taste good and feel right, and we're willing for them to become a part of us.

▸ We may also want to keep in mind that language is always somewhat removed from what it describes, that there are many valid ways of slicing the same pie, and that verbal misunderstandings are a common fixture of human affairs. So I appeal to my readers to be patient, to maintain open minds, and to give any unfamiliar notions a fair hearing before giving them a thumbs-up, a thumbs-down, or a healthy "maybe."

▸ This book is partly a collection of individual essays. I've sequenced them to provide as much flow and continuity as possible and hopefully connect enough of the right dots in the most meaningful and useful ways. To keep things accessible I've done my best to avoid overly technical or specialized language.

▸ This book is divided into three main parts:
  ▪ In Part I we will survey the emerging fields of afterlife research and related studies.
  ▪ In Part II we will examine in detail some of the most carefully studied and scientifically robust evidence for an afterlife.
  ▪ In Part III we will consider the substance, location, experience, and purpose of an afterlife, and its relevance to our earthly lives.
  ▪ A resources section and recommended reading list provide further information and perspectives on the question of an afterlife.

Now let's fasten our mental seat belts and prepare to take a deep dive into one of today's most compelling and far-reaching frontiers of scientific exploration.

PART I

Getting Oriented

1

Materialism 101

To most educated people in our modern Western world, including many of the most aware, intelligent, and compassionate secular humanists, the notion of an afterlife makes no sense at all. Obviously the physical body dies, and that's the end of it. Poof! Gone!

So in what possible fabric of reality could our existence continue? Wouldn't any such notion smack of archaic religious belief or "New-Age woo-woo"? After all, mainstream science, academia, and our dominant Western culture have long insisted that the whole of reality includes only a single domain. It is fundamentally mechanistic, deterministic, and limited to what can be perceived by our bodily senses or detected and measured by instruments we ourselves have devised.

This belief system is known as "materialism."* Materialism asserts, explicitly or implicitly, that:

- We exist in a "dead" universe—a framework of lifeless, soulless matter, energy, space, and tick-tock time. There is no deeper, more

---

*Materialism, in this sense, is also known as "physicalism" and "mechanistic reductionism"—the assumption that all of life and consciousness can ultimately be reduced to a dead, deterministic physics. It is closely related to "scientism"—the view that science equals materialistic science and that it alone can discern truth about the world and reality. "Scientism" can also mean putting a sciency spin on things to lend them a certain authority.

encompassing, or more alive reality in any sense. Any evidence that suggests such a reality must be ignored or rejected out of hand as erroneous, fictitious, or fraudulent.

- Our universe and our natural environment consist of purely mechanistic "parts" or "building blocks" governed by fixed laws. They are therefore incapable of originality, creative volition, or purpose. Despite the nonexistence of magic, these purposeless parts magically "self-organize" and demonstrate inexplicably higher-order "emergent properties" when enough of them happen to get together and rub elbows. (Philosophers call this "upward causation." The general idea is that if enough bricks put their heads together they could create a beautiful and structurally sophisticated building.)

- There is no essential distinction between lifeless and living matter other than chemistry and relative complexity. We haven't done it yet, but we're firm in our faith that someday we will create living organisms from inanimate matter in some godlike fashion. After all, we believe that it's only a matter of the right interactions of the right parts under the right conditions.

- The entire course of biological evolution in all its incalculable diversity, including the emergence of sentient creatures, is fully accounted for by chance interactions aided by natural selection—the survival of the fittest, most numerous, most fortuitously adaptable, or nastiest. The sudden appearance of new species following global extinction events and the recently acknowledged phenomenon of rapid evolution are no exception.

- The ultimate purposes of knowledge are prediction, control, and the exploitation of nature.

- Imagination, creativity, and free will can be fully explained as random events. Intention can be fully accounted for in terms of selfishness and physical survival.

- Consciousness has no fundamental reality of its own. It's only a mysterious byproduct of electrophysiological activity within the human brain.* Actual experiences (awareness, emotion, insight, foresight, appreciation, aversion, volition, love, and so on—not to mention the very experience of selfhood itself) are considered *epi*-phenomena—illusions.†

- We, and all living creatures, are genetically programmed biological machines destined to the trash heap of physical decay. We are unsustainable and essentially disposable.
- When our bodies and brains expire or meet untimely ends our streams of experience simply cease.
- Since subjective experience is entirely insubstantial, outward behavior is the most logical basis for understanding and applying human psychology. (In most academic and therapeutic environments, psychology is considered a *behavioral* rather than *experiential* science.)
- According to post-humanist‡ materialists, our inner, subjective self, if any, consists purely of "information," which is purportedly stored in some finite fashion within our physical brains. So if that information were somehow digitized and downloaded into computers we would become immortal and continue to experience our illusory existence.§ (Would a duplicate copy of the data be equally sentient and have its own independent illusory identity?)

---

*The assumption that the brain causes consciousness has been likened to the assumption that firefighters cause fires. It's actually quite logical since firefighters are normally seen around fires, and the larger the fire, the more firefighters are seen. It's a no-brainer!

†To what, or to whom, these illusions appear is apparently never considered!

‡The term "post-humanism" or "posthumanism" (not to be confused with post-materialism) has several meanings—see Wikipedia. In this context it refers to the enhancement and/or eventual replacement of humans by artificial intelligence.

§Some fellow-traveler materialists have had their bodies, or just their heads or brains, injected with preservatives and deep-frozen, trusting that they'll be born again as soon as materialistic science, in its infinite resourcefulness, discovers how to defrost them, revive them, and perform the needed transplants. One company that provides this service is the Alcor Life Extension Foundation. You can read more about them in Wikipedia.

- The only alternative to mainstream science is mainstream religion. The alphabet of possibilities runs all the way from A to B.
- Life is ultimately meaningless.

That, in a nutshell, is the picture of reality, which, for more than four centuries, has weighed on popular and academic Western thought with a heavy, invisible hand. It has therefore determined many of our modern world's unquestioned assumptions about life and death and has deeply influenced our collective priorities.

Materialism as a Way of Life

Our modern world's dominant value system is also known as "materialism." As a way of life it exalts material goods, conveniences and luxuries, and the means of acquiring them. Often the means become ends in themselves. Sometimes the mere *appearance* of means becomes the very purpose of life!

This philosophy may be as shallow as it gets, but it makes perfect sense if you believe that matter* is all there is and that death is the end. The old joke that "the guy who dies with the most toys wins" is no joke. Get yours while you can, keeping in mind that your "net worth" is denominated in dollars. Many of our culture's most influential role models seem to live proudly by these assumptions and do their best to put them into practice.

Materialism as Religion

I think the evidence is compelling that this "worship of building blocks" has become a de facto planetary religion, implicitly dictating the limits of reality and offering pseudosalvation to the highest bidder. This edifice of faith has profoundly influenced our civilization's approach to

---

*"Matter" is intended here as shorthand for matter, energy, space, and time. These are the four interdependent foundations of physical reality as we normally perceive and understand it. However, our materialistic cultural bias tends to focus our attention primarily on matter.

everything from economics to ecology, education, social order, medicine, and politics, not to mention birth, life, and death.

So why is our world blind to other possibilities? Arguably for the same reason that fish are said to be unaware of water: Since it's all they have ever known, how could they possibly suspect the existence of anything else? Water is simply "reality," and rumors of a world populated by air-breathing creatures must seem the stuff of sheerest fantasy. A skeptical fish would scoff at such outlandish claims, tiptail around them, and surely refuse to investigate rumors of such unthinkable things. After all, a fish has a family to feed and a reputation to protect!

Silly, perhaps. But is it any less silly than our confusing the material world with reality as a whole and dismissing any possibility of further exploration?

Obviously a healthy understanding and command of our material world can be genuinely beneficial. But in mistaking lifeless matter for the underlying foundation of reality we systematically undermine our planet's health and sustainability. When our life-support system—the living environment—takes a back seat to so many lifeless things, is it unthinkable that the eventual outcome could be a lifeless planet?

> *Without a biosphere in a good shape, there is no life on the planet. It's very simple. That's all you need to know.*
>
> VACLAV SMIL, SCIENTIST AND
> AUTHOR OF *GROWTH*

Yet another facet of materialistic science is the "war-machine" model of attacking bacterial diseases with increasingly powerful antibiotics. This has inevitably bred drug-resistant strains of microbes, and one of the few things mechanistic science can do about this is to escalate the battle by coming up with more powerful weapons. This philosophy of "martial medicine" closely parallels the practice of modern chemical agriculture, in which the nutrient-rich, life-sustaining complexity of natural soils is destroyed, creating a fragile dependency on the industrial production of synthetic fertilizers and toxic pesticides and herbicides.

Finally, if we are nothing but our physical bodies and death is the end, then murder, war, and suicide offer appealing ways of solving our problems forever. If we don't get caught, voted out of office, or dissuaded at the last moment, it's a done deal, with no need to consider ultimate consequences or accountability.

So, enough! If this all feels a bit heavy, why don't we pause, take a deep breath of fresh air, and imagine for a moment how a *post*-materialist worldview might look and feel, how it would affect our sense of reality, and how it would impact our individual and social lives.

> *Expose your mental models to the open air.*
>
> DONELLA MEADOWS,
> ENVIRONMENTAL SCIENTIST

For starters, would we have to abandon the scientific approach? Let's take a look.

Materialism vs. Science

Does science necessarily equal materialism? Short answer: No. *Science is a method of inquiry* while materialism is *an assumption about reality—a belief or presupposition that is simply accepted by default.*

One result of this confusion is that mountains of robust evidence for a more inclusive picture of reality are commonly ignored, casually explained away, or naively swept under the rug as being "unscientific." So labeled, there they remain, if not entirely invisible then at least off-limits to most serious researchers eager to bring their curiosity and their best means and methods, including logic, to the table.

Could afterlife research be perfectly logical? Well, logic is a tool, and a tool cuts whichever way you point it. So if evidence of an afterlife presents itself, doesn't logic itself dictate that it should be brought to bear on the evidence evenhandedly, because then we might learn something valuable? To refuse or avoid doing so on grounds of stubborn disbelief alone would seem to be profoundly illogical and radically unscientific.

> *The more we push puzzles away, the bigger they tend to grow and grow.*
>
> PETER KINGSLEY,
> WRITER AND PHILOSOPHER

For the past century, relativity, quantum mechanics, and countless theories du jour have shaken the foundations of classical physics. Quantum entanglement, for example, confirms nonlocality (what Einstein called "spooky action at a distance"), which transcends spacetime as we normally understand it. The classic double-slit experiment* appears to demonstrate that conscious intention can directly affect physical systems. String theory proposes, in part, that the vibration of a mysterious, fundamental *something* may be the ultimate source of physical reality.† Yet such insights have been slow to trickle down into the mainstream, and those who might acknowledge them tend to face hurricane-force headwinds of peer pressure and disapproval. Thus the deeply rooted materialistic bias of mainstream science continues to decree that our awareness must be an illusory *effect* and cannot possibly be a root *cause* of anything at all. So blind physical forces are held to reign supreme, and consciousness remains effectively excluded from any fundamental role in the scheme of things.

---

*If you haven't heard of this experiment, Dean Radin's 2016 talk posted to YouTube, "New Experiments Show Consciousness Affects Matter," at the IONS Science of Consciousness Conference, provides a good overview (posted by the Institute of Noetic Sciences on June 7, 2016).

†If you're unfamiliar with string theory, take 2.5 minutes to watch Brian Green's explanation on YouTube. See "What Is String Theory?" (posted by the World Science Festival on July 25, 2019).

So Is There No Way Out of This Dead End?

As we shall see, there is indeed a way out. It has been found by a growing cadre of courageous researchers who have risked sticking their necks out and raised profound questions about the materialistic model of reality. Many of these questions are based on strong experimental results and robust empirical evidence.

So the work of post-materialist science is already underway. Please read on.

Science is a method of inquiry, not an ideology. Today there are many scientists who believe in materialism; but that is a belief structure or a philosophy, and science is a method of inquiry—it doesn't have to be committed to a particular worldview.

RUPERT SHELDRAKE, PH.D.,
BIOLOGIST, AUTHOR

At each shift of the paradigm, the impossible presents its impeccable credentials . . . and the unthinkable becomes the norm.

RABBI MICHAEL BERG

Discovery begins with the awareness of anomaly.

THOMAS KUHN IN HIS SEMINAL WORK,
THE STRUCTURE OF SCIENTIFIC REVOLUTIONS

All truth passes through three stages. First, it is ridiculed. Second, it is violently opposed. Third, it is accepted as being self-evident.

ARTHUR SCHOPENHAUER, PHILOSOPHER

There are more things in heaven and earth, Horatio, than are dreamt of in your philosophy.

WILLIAM SHAKESPEARE, *HAMLET*

Chapter 1 Summary

- We live in a world dominated by a belief in materialism.
- Science is a method of inquiry; materialism is an assumption about reality.
- Social pressures and militant skepticism tend to inhibit post-materialist thinking and research.
- A paradigm shift into post-materialism is underway.

2

The Landscape of Afterlife Research

In recent decades, several branches of afterlife research have emerged into public awareness. Though each tends to have its own special focus, taken together they form a compelling body of evidence for the existence of a supra-physical realm in which our "essence" or "deep self" lives, moves, and has its being beyond the boundaries of our physical lives.

This realm appears to be at least as fundamentally real as our familiar physical universe. But ironically, its underlying substance appears to be something we normally regard as insubstantial: *consciousness*. This "substance," though apparently anchored in a higher "octave of reality," can interact with the familiar physical universe most obviously through our brains and bodies, but perhaps also in other ways, as we shall see.

So what do we mean by "octaves of reality"?

Musical pitches (frequencies of physical vibration that we can hear through the air or feel as they travel through solid matter) are organized into octaves—each octave being a series of eight notes representing a doubling or halving of frequency. The lowest A on a piano vibrates about 27 times per second and the highest at about 3,500 times per second. Quite a difference. But while a piano string has to be physically struck in order to vibrate, physical matter and energy at the most microscopic scale are always vibrating. For example, oxygen atoms vibrate 60 billion times per second. Light, being more subtle than matter, vibrates much more rapidly: visible light vibrates about 5 quadrillion times per second! One appealing speculation is that consciousness and its forms (thoughts, images, feelings, and the whole gamut of experience) are subtler yet, and may therefore vibrate at rates that are so many octaves higher than physical matter that the two cannot normally interact. The main exception would be through sensitive biological and neurological processes. This might be one way of looking at the most deeply fundamental difference between nonliving and living matter. It might also explain how consciousness can appear to be produced by the brain. Taking this further, if consciousness is as imaginative and creative as it appears to be, one might speculate that as a higher-frequency phenomenon it may spin off lower-frequency undertones, including the matter and energy that constitute the familiar physical realm.

> *If you want to find the secrets of the universe, think in terms of energy, frequency and vibration.*
>
> Nikola Tesla, inventor and visionary

So are we witnessing the birth of a new scientific trajectory? Should there be any doubt, here are several robust examples, some of which will be elaborated in the following chapters.

Near-Death Experience Research

By the mid-twentieth century, modern medicine inadvertently began to cast some doubt on the materialistic view of life and death, as it could now resuscitate many clinically dead people who would otherwise have remained clinically dead.

Contrary to all expectation, some of these fortunate folks reported complex, coherent, lucid experiences that took place while their bodies were flatlined and with zero detectable brain activity* for significant

---

*Recommended memoirs are Anita Moorjani's *Dying to Be Me,* Mellen-Thomas Benedict's *Journey through the Light and Back,* and Eben Alexander's *Proof of Heaven.*

periods of time—sometimes hours. These included perfectly clear perceptions of their immediate and *extended* physical surroundings (down the hall, around the corner, outside the building . . .) from "impossible" points of view and the ability to accurately describe what they saw and heard there. Some reported being "tuned out" of their familiar surroundings into a nonmaterial realm that seemed to offer degrees of freedom and types of experience unavailable to them in their embodied lives. Some reported profound encounters with presences sometimes perceived as respected individuals or personal guides, as well as deceased friends, family members, and even pets. In some cases these near-death experiencers (NDErs) were apparently able to bring back verifiable information to be conveyed to complete strangers from *their* family members on the other side. Equally striking, some NDErs reported encounters with deceased relatives they didn't know had died or of whom they had had no previous knowledge at all.

These experiences were nearly always described as love-infused and blissful. Curiously, they were almost universally characterized as "more real" than those of their physical lives. Sometimes they included extended perceptions, such as colors, music, and concepts not normally encompassed by our physical senses and everyday minds. Some, who had "never had a mathematical bone in their body," reported having a clear and easy grasp of higher mathematical concepts. In a few cases, individuals blind from birth reported accurate visual perception of their physical surroundings.*

Another common feature of these near-death experiences (NDEs) was a stopping point at which experiencers addressed their return to embodied life. In most cases they were advised that their time hadn't come yet and that they must return to their physical bodies to live out their present life "as planned." In other instances they were presented with a choice: return to your existing—often severely damaged—body, or be reborn in a new body. Other experiencers were told that they

---

Mindsight, by Kenneth Ring, Ph.D., and Sharon Cooper, explores this fascinating aspect of the NDE.

could stay if they chose to, but they opted to return to physical life for the sake of others, typically their children.

Surprisingly, their return—even to a badly damaged or seriously ill body—was almost invariably followed by profound, permanent, positive transformations of their personalities, values, and life purpose. Such outcomes are unlikely to be attributable to random fantasies, hallucinations, or mental disorders, let alone grave physical injury or illness.

Nonetheless, these reports were at first dismissed as the delusional products of oxygen-starved brains, powerful medications, or anesthesia. (Some still are, by hardened skeptics who remain stubbornly unfamiliar with the depth and scope of the available data.)

By the mid-1970s, however, this growing body of reports could no longer be dismissed quite so casually, and credible investigators with impeccable professional and academic credentials began to study it systematically. They concluded that no materialistic explanations could be stretched far enough to account for these reported experiences.

Concurrently, numerous scientific reports and books appeared on the scene, notably Dr. Elisabeth Kübler-Ross's groundbreaking *On Death and Dying* (1969) and Dr. Raymond Moody's *Life After Life* (1975), which made the notion of the survival of consciousness* more thinkable, whether or not conventional beliefs and theories could account for it.

Over time, this trend opened a window through which experiencers' reports could be further evaluated by growing numbers of scientists and academics. It also fostered an atmosphere in which NDErs could discuss their experiences more openly and with less fear of harmful repercussions. Too often these have included social rejection,

---

*The phrase "survival of consciousness" can be somewhat misleading in implying that consciousness originates in the physical body and then continues beyond physical death. It neglects to recognize the evidence for the existence of consciousness prior to incarnation.

"labeling,"* skeptical ridicule, professional and familial ostracism, clerical condemnation, and forced commitment to psychiatric institutions.

In 1978 a group of scientists, doctors, and academics† founded the International Association for Near-Death Studies (IANDS), the first organization devoted to the systematic study of near-death and related experiences. Today its members hail from every continent but Antarctica.

According to Dr. Bruce Greyson at the University of Virginia, the phenomenon of the NDE had been recorded by a variety of ancient cultures, including Tibet, India, Egypt, China, and Japan. Mention of the NDE is also found in the Bible, in the writings of Plato, and in the folklore of Pacific Islanders and Native Americans. In more modern times it appeared in nineteenth-century French medical journals, in which terms analogous to "near-death experience" were first coined.

Perhaps the single most exhaustive and scientifically compelling study of the NDE was conducted between 1988 and 1992 by Dutch cardiologist Pim van Lommel. It was a controlled, prospective study that involved 344 successive patients who had been declared clinically dead and were subsequently resuscitated. Dr. Van Lommel's study, "Getting Comfortable With Near-Death Experiences: Dutch Prospective Research on Near-Death Experiences During Cardiac Arrest," was first published in the *Lancet* in 2001, and later elaborated in his 2010 book, *Consciousness Beyond Life.*

---

*When, in a few notable instances, following an NDE the individual's terminal condition, such as cancer, completely disappeared, the opaque, dismissive label "spontaneous remission" seemed to serve in lieu of any actual investigation. Case closed! Again I point you to Anita Moorjani's *Dying to Be Me,* Mellen-Thomas Benedict's *Journey through the Light and Back,* and Eben Alexander's *Proof of Heaven.*

†IANDS was cofounded by John Audette, Dr. Raymond Moody, Dr. Kenneth Ring, Dr. Bruce Greyson, and Dr. Michael Sabom. More information about the founders can be found on the IANDS website.

Near-death experiencers are the wonder workers of modern times, leading us into an entirely new understanding of and relationship with our own souls. They challenge us to revisit our entire approach to death and dying.

WHITLEY STRIEBER, AUTHOR

Reincarnation Research

Meanwhile, other fields of research began to question whether our awareness and sense of self are in fact manufactured by our brains: Could these instead be *interacting* with our brains for the duration of one or more lifetimes, much as continuous radio waves interact with physical communication devices that come and go?

In 1967, Ian Stevenson, the chair of the University of Virginia Medical School's Department of Psychiatry, established a research unit now named the Division of Perceptual Studies (DOPS). It was initially funded by Chester Carlson, the inventor of the Xerox photocopier, and was dedicated to "researching what, if anything, of the human personality survives death." Dr. Stevenson himself went on to research hundreds of accounts of young children who claimed to recall past lives, producing an impressive body of evidence that strongly favored the continuity of individual identity from one physical lifetime to another. The late Dr. Stevenson's work has been continued by his colleagues, Drs. Jim Tucker and Bruce Greyson.[*]

To many observers, reincarnation appears to offer the most elegantly logical explanation for baffling anomalies that present far too early in life to be accounted for in any conventional way. These include inexplicable talents, phobias, mastery of unlearned languages, advanced IQs, and declarations of opposite-gender orientation.

Similarly, in many instances a subject's present body may bear blemishes and deformities that coincide precisely with the sites of documented injuries in a claimed past life.

---

[*]An excellent hour-long retrospective video on their work can be found on YouTube, titled "Is There Life after Death? Fifty Years of Research at UVA" (posted by UVA Medical Center Hour on March 7, 2017).

Perhaps the most extensively researched modern American case of reincarnation is that of young James Leininger. In his most recent life James had apparently been James Huston, a U.S. Navy pilot who had been shot down over the Sea of Japan during World War II. His outstandingly evidential story has appeared in several television documentaries and is chronicled in the book *Soul Survivor.* We take a deeper dive into the Leininger reincarnation case in chapter 8.

Life-between-Lives Research

In the 1970s Michael Newton, Ph.D., a conventionally trained clinical hypnotherapist, noted that during deep-hypnosis sessions some of his clients reported apparent memories of experiences between lifetimes. Skeptical at first, he dismissed these reports as products of his clients' imaginations. But after noticing unlikely consistencies among them he was compelled to adopt a more scientific approach. After recording and analyzing his clients' sessions he eventually pieced together a detailed picture of their between-lives experiences. His work came to fruition in his two remarkable books, *Journey of Souls* and *Destiny of Souls,* as well as through a network of practitioners who continue his work with their own clients.

Afterlife Communication through Modern Electronics

Back in the 1950s, when audiotape recorders first became available as consumer items, users occasionally reported hearing faint voices of unknown origin in their recordings. In the United States these were generally dismissed as radio broadcasts being randomly picked up by the recorder's electronics. But in Europe a number of physicists, engineers, psychologists, and experimenters did take this Electronic Voice Phenomenon (EVP) seriously. Soon they had demonstrated effective communication from the departed via radio, telephone, sound recording devices, and eventually computers, fax machines, and video systems. They concluded that certain individuals on the other side seemed to be able to bring their conscious intention to bear on our electronic devices well enough to communicate with our physical world in an objective, repeatable way. These researchers then sought to understand and optimize these communications through continued experimentation. This practice, known as Instrumental Trans-Communication (ITC), flourished in the 1980s and '90s and quietly continues today, mainly in Europe, the United States, and Brazil. It is described in greater detail in chapter 6.

Mental Mediumship Research

A natural communication practice, acknowledged for millennia but newly revived, is known as "mental mediumship." Mental mediums essentially act as living intermediaries for the consciousness of those on the other side and can deliver detailed, verifiable information, sometimes previously unknown to anyone alive.

Mediumistic talent includes a spectrum of abilities. The simplest and most common is the ability to receive mental impressions from the other side and express or *channel* them as direct speech or as written words (often termed "automatic writing"). At the other extreme, some mediums are able to let their own consciousness step aside and permit another's to fully inhabit and animate their bodies. This is known as "full trance channeling."

Skeptics tend to believe mediumship is impossible and must therefore be a matter of trickery—usually "cold reading." This is a technique in which a fraudulent medium asks leading questions and observes a subject's emotional reactions to suggestive phrases and so is able to fabricate plausible "messages" to impress the subject. These and other deceptive practices have been carefully ruled out in rigorous studies of mediums' brainwave patterns at the Institute of Noetic Sciences in Petaluma, California, at the Windbridge Institute in Tucson, Arizona, and in other studies.*

---

*Three of these other studies include Bastos Jr., et al., "Frontal Electroencephalographic (EEG) Activity and Mediumship"; Delorme, "Electrocortical Activity Associated with Subjective Communication with the Deceased"; and Hageman, et al., "The Neurobiology of Trance and Mediumship in Brazil." (Further details for all scientific articles are given in the recommended reading list.)

As it happens, one of today's most talented, prolific, and evidential mental mediums, Suzanne Giesemann, is a retired U.S. Navy commander and former aide to the chairman of the Joint Chiefs of Staff.

Involuntary Mediumship and Post-mortem Pranks

Do we all possess some mediumistic talent? This notion is supported by the phenomenon of *spontaneous* or *involuntary* mediumship.

When a loved one passes on, those left behind often report experiences of their loved one's presence in the form of inner impressions, thoughts, words, tactile sensations, aromas, visitations, and various phenomena that are unmistakably linked with the departed individual. Often dismissed as wishful imaginings or hallucinations, these events appear to be more common, robust, and compelling than is generally acknowledged. Sometimes the deceased person presents at the foot of a loved one's bed, with the percipient fully awake; often a lengthy, coherent conversation may ensue. Two personal acquaintances of mine have been astonished and delighted by departed friends' quasi-physical appearance in the passenger seats of their cars.

Then there is the baffling phenomenon of the full materialization of deceased persons. I myself had tended to dismiss such reports until one day in December 1967 I met and shook hands with Joe, a friend of a friend who, we later learned, had been dead for two years. There was nothing about this person's presence that seemed at all unusual or unnatural. He was tall, had a thick mustache, and was well dressed. What I recall most about him was the firmness of his handshake. Curiously, Joe had suddenly shown up after an absence of some years and following this visit was untraceable.

Commonly reported "pranks" pulled by the deceased include switching lights and other electrical devices on and off, and the displacement, appearance, and disappearance of small objects. I have experienced these myself on a number of occasions and with appropriate skepticism eliminated all mundane possibilities before considering them genuinely anomalous.

There is a considerable body of lore surrounding these types of phenomena that begs to be researched and analyzed rigorously and without prejudice. Are they wholly or partly a form of involuntary mediumship* on the part of the percipients? At this point we simply don't know. Hopefully as the stigma attached to these experiences diminishes we'll be in a better position to investigate them on a level scientific playing field.

The Ouija Board

This popular device for communicating with nonphysical entities appears to be a sort of psychological crutch, enabling its users to overcome their own disbelief by projecting their success onto an external object. Its downside is that dabblers and casual curiosity seekers may not always be selective enough in their intentions and can be misled by "unevolved spirits" bearing false or frightening narratives or manipulative information.

Physical Mediumship

Physical mediumship seeks to create conditions in which the departed can bring their consciousness to bear directly on the physical world, producing hard evidence that can be preserved or recorded for further study. While this practice has often been subjected to scornful skepticism—and occasional fraud by unscrupulous practitioners—some modern efforts have passed critical scientific scrutiny with flying colors. By far the most successful was the five-year experiment conducted in the English town of Scole in the late 1990s. The Scole Experiment was chronicled in two books, a 300-page scientific report, and a full-length documentary film.

This experiment, which yielded an unprecedented variety of physical evidence, was witnessed and monitored for over two years by a

---

*Some researchers have suggested that multiple personality disorder might be an extreme form of involuntary mediumship. For two examples, see Braude, "Mediumship and Multiple Personality" and Kluft, "Commentary on 'Multiple Personality and Channeling.'"

team of experienced investigators well trained in exposing trickery and fraud. Over the five-year course of the experiment, hundreds of visitors attended the Scole sessions. At no time was any evidence of deception detected.

We take a closer look at the Scole Experiment in chapter 7.

Out-of-Body Experiences

In 1958 a New York radio producer, Robert Monroe, began having spontaneous out-of-body experiences (OBEs) not associated with any illness or accident. Concerned for his sanity, he underwent a battery of examinations but was deemed in perfect physical and mental health. Informed by a psychiatrist friend that other cultures prized such an ability, he was encouraged to nurture it. In due course he developed techniques that allowed him, and eventually others, to visit and navigate nonphysical realms, including those reported by NDErs and deceased individuals communicating from the other side. His legacy includes three books: *Journeys Out of the Body, Far Journeys,* and *Ultimate Journey.* He also founded the Monroe Institute in Charlottesville, Virginia, which continues his work and teaches his techniques. Others, including author William Buhlman and the Portugal-based International Academy of Consciousness, have developed a variety of approaches and techniques for inducing and navigating OBEs.

The Bigelow Institute Competition

In June 2020 aerospace entrepreneur and consciousness researcher Robert Bigelow founded the Bigelow Institute for Consciousness Studies "to support research into both the survival of human consciousness after physical death and, based on data from such studies, the nature of the afterlife."

In January 2021 Bigelow launched an essay competition offering awards totaling 1 million U.S. dollars for anyone who could demonstrate the existence of life after death. The outcome was a novel body of work: 204 essays on the best evidence for an afterlife, from which twenty-nine winners were chosen. The authors included eight M.D.s and twenty Ph.D.s.*

The winning essays can be downloaded from the website of the Bigelow Institute for Consciousness. At this writing (winter 2022–23) the institute has launched additional competitions aimed at developing further experimental proofs of the afterlife and techniques for reliable communication with the departed.

> *We should be devoting enormous social resources to this question [of survival], not leaving it up to a matter of belief.*
>
> CHARLES T. TART, PH.D., PROFESSOR EMERITUS,
> UNIVERSITY OF CALIFORNIA, DAVIS

Chapter 2 Summary

The landscape of afterlife research includes:

- Near-Death Experience research
- Reincarnation research
- Life-between-lives research
- Instrumental Trans-Communication research and practice
- Mental mediumship research and practice
- Physical mediumship research and practice
- Out-of-Body Experience research and practice
- Diverse avenues of research represented by the twenty-nine winning Bigelow Institute essays

---

*The judges included Jeffrey J. Kripal, Ph.D., associate dean at Rice University; journalist Leslie Kean; neurophysiologist Christopher C. Green, M.D., Ph.D.; Brian Weiss, M.D., chairman emeritus of psychiatry at the Mount Sinai Medical Center in Miami; Jessica Utts, Ph.D., past president of the American Statistical Association; and physicist-researcher Harold Puthoff, Ph.D.

3

Supportive Studies in Related Phenomena

There is a spectrum of phenomena not normally associated with after-life research per se, but which are intriguing in their own right and support the validity of a consciousness-based, post-materialist worldview. They include the following.

Savant Research

Autistic savants* are individuals who can perform astounding feats of memory and pull astronomically challenging mathematical solutions out of thin air. Though once known pejoratively as "idiot savants," these people are hardly idiots. They seem to have instant access to worlds of information not learned by conventional means, and some appear to be adept at telepathic communication. Some of these individuals are challenged by hydrocephalus—their brain cavities are disproportionately filled with fluid and contain significantly diminished brain tissue.

These facts tend to support the post-materialist notion that the brain, rather than being the source of consciousness, may be acting as

---

*Some of the most fascinating and outstanding research on savants has been pursued by Oregon-based neuroscientist Diane Hennacy Powell, M.D. Her presentation, "Autistic Savants and Their Radical Implications for Neuroscience," can be viewed on YouTube (posted by FMBRTV on July 8, 2021).

a transmitter-receiver or relay station that is narrowly tuned to specific frequencies or patterns of consciousness. This highly selective tuning would effectively make the brain what some researchers have called a "reducing valve" or "focusing device" that normally funnels our waking awareness toward our bodily and worldly experiences to the exclusion of all else. According to this model, particular kinds of diminished cerebral capacity would tend to make the brain less narrowly selective in its tuning, allowing it to connect more easily and naturally with other sources of input and layers or realms of consciousness. These may include the *akasha,* which Eastern philosophies identify as the universal repository or "central server" of all memory.

Terminal Lucidity

Persons with severe, irreversible brain damage have often demonstrated periods of clear presence and perfectly normal mental functioning shortly before death. This has been termed "terminal lucidity." It suggests that an afflicted brain can sometimes "get out of the way" before its demise completely severs the connection between the person's body and their surviving consciousness. This appears to support the notion that the brain puts defining limits on the functioning of normal human consciousness. According to biologist Rupert Sheldrake, observations suggest that terminal lucidity may also occur in domestic animals.

The Shared-Death Experience

Another deathbed-related phenomenon, known as the Shared-Death Experience (SDE), can occur as a dying person leaves their body. Sometimes a caregiver or loved one at their bedside will suddenly experience accompanying the dying person partway or entirely into the "welcoming" stage of their afterlife. While this can be a shock to those who may have had no belief in such a thing, many SDE experiencers have reported profound transformations in their worldviews and their attitudes toward death.*

---

*See the excellent research report on the SDE by the Shared Crossing Research Initiative titled "Shared Death Experiences." Also google "Shared Crossing Project."

Psychedelics, Entheogens, and Empathogens

Lately certain psychedelic ("mind-manifesting"), entheogenic ("spirit-generating"), and empathogenic ("love-generating") plants and chemical substances, long regarded by our Western culture as dangerous hallucinogens lacking any benefits, are being progressively legalized and have become objects of legitimate medical and psychological research. Traditional cultures have long prized such substances as tools for reconnecting an individual's consciousness with aspects of the Greater Reality. Now a psychedelic renaissance is underway, and Western science is beginning to get the message: these substances can apparently dilate the brain's focus, soften its hard "spotlight beam," and grant one's consciousness greater liberty to explore beyond our limited physical senses and restrictive cultural conditioning. For this reason, some are now being used—with expert guidance—to aid the release of long-held traumas and even to ease the transition to physical death.

It should be noted that, as with autistic savants and terminal lucidity, psychedelics appear to liberate perception as a function of *diminished* brain activity.*

Lucid Dreaming

Lucid dreaming is a state in which dreamers are consciously aware that they are dreaming. This can occur spontaneously or as a result of intention and practice. Skilled lucid dreamers can control their dreams and can create and participate in "other realities" at will, creating "virtual environments" in which personal interactions and analogues of physical activity can take place, exactly as reported by NDErs and by those who communicate from the afterlife.

---

*Supportive studies include: Halberstadt and Geyer, "Do Psychedelics Expand the Mind by Reducing Brain Activity?"; Costandi, "Psychedelic Chemical Subdues Brain Activity"; and Carhart-Harris, et al., "Neural Correlates of the LSD Experience Revealed by Multimodal Neuroimaging."

Lucid dreaming supports the view that conscious intentionality can function independently of the waking mind, if not the physical body and brain.* Some lucid dreamers have reported achieving profound psychological healing—for example from ADHD, chronic nightmares, and so forth. In some cases the remission of physiological conditions, including but not limited to chemical addictions, has apparently been achieved as well. Some lucid dreamers have reported vividly reexperiencing details of past lives in considerable detail. Others believe that the practice† can prepare us for navigating and taking responsibility for our projected sense of reality in the afterlife.

If you're interested in learning to become a lucid dreamer, please note: as with any practices and substances that introduce us to navigating the farther reaches of consciousness, it is wisest, safest, and most effective to approach lucid dreaming by working with a qualified, experienced practitioner.

The Placebo Effect

Materialistic medicine tends to deny the power of the mind to significantly influence our physical health. Yet clinical trials of "miracle" drugs must grapple with the placebo effect, which may perform "miracle" cures that can skew the trial results!

Precognition and Presentiment

These are phenomena in which effects precede their own causes, suggesting that time's role in the fabric of reality may not always be what we assume it to be. From a mechanistic perspective, precognition (pre-seeing) or presentiment (pre-feeling) would seem to make no sense. But such reversals of time's direction have been demonstrated in a number

---

*According to Robert Waggoner, author of *Lucid Dreaming: Gateway to the Inner Self* and coauthor with Caroline McCready of *Lucid Dreaming: Plain and Simple,* skeptics considered lucid dreaming nonsense until 1975, when it was confirmed by brainwave research.
†The online magazine *The Lucid Dreaming Experience* is a free, reader-supported, quarterly magazine devoted to all aspects of lucid dreaming and its related experiences.

of ways. For example, in rigorously controlled experiments, subjects have been shown randomized, randomly timed photographs with a range of emotional content that triggers predictable brainwave patterns. In instances far beyond chance these subjects register the expected responses moments *before* being shown the relevant photos.*

Precognitive dreams and visions are not uncommon. My own precognitive dreams at an early age played a key role in jump-starting my lifelong interest in these phenomena and the questions they raise about the nature of consciousness and reality.

J. W. Dunne, a pioneering British aircraft designer in the early twentieth century, was intrigued by consciousness and developed his own theories about its nature. In his classic book *An Experiment with Time,* he describes a simple experiment anyone can do to induce precognitive dreams. I have tried this experiment myself and experienced remarkable results. Dunne's book is still in print, so why not pick up a copy and try it yourself?

Clairvoyance, or Remote Viewing

These involve the ability to view, in the mind's eye, remote places and events in real time. For example, during the Cold War the CIA and the U.S. Army funded experiments† based on disciplined remote-viewing protocols that yielded impressively accurate, actionable intelligence.

Map Dowsing

A related talent is known as "map dowsing," in which remote targets are intuited in terms of locations on a map. My personal experience

---

*See Bem, et al., "Feeling the Future."

†Professor of statistics Jessica Utts explains in a talk posted to YouTube, "Remote Viewing and Statistical Validation" (posted by Beach TC CSULB on March 26, 2018), that consistency observed in remote-viewing experiments is supported by robust statistical analysis. The 2019 documentary film *Third Eye Spies* provides a revealing peek behind the curtain of official secrecy that had once surrounded these highly classified projects.

includes a situation in which the location of a stolen musical instrument was successfully pinponted to within a two-block radius in the San Francisco Bay Area, an urban region with a population of about 8 million, covering 7,000 square miles. The dowser in this case was the legendary Harold McCoy.*

Telepathy

Telepathy is another one of those phenomena that, according to the materialistic paradigm, cannot possibly occur. Yet careful experiments in human and animal telepathy have proven surprisingly successful. Perhaps the most exhaustive series of rigorously controlled and monitored telepathy experiments is chronicled in Rupert Sheldrake's classic, best-selling book *Dogs That Know When Their Owners Are Coming Home.*

> *Maybe it's a superstition; maybe it really happens. The only way to find out is to study the phenomenon and find out whether it happens or not. Not to adopt the view that it's a superstition and then close off any inquiry. That way we find out nothing. We remain trapped in our belief system.*
>
> RUPERT SHELDRAKE, PH.D.,
> BIOLOGIST, AUTHOR

> *If you just go "lalalalala, I'm right and you're wrong" when dismissing something literally thousands of people have reported, rather than trying to actually find out what's causing it, you're not a scientist. You're a smug twit.*
>
> A YOUTUBE COMMENT,
> PARAPHRASED

---

*Harold McCoy was profiled in *Living Now* magazine in 2005 in the article "Power of the Focused Mind," which is available online.

Chapter 3 Summary

Extensively studied phenomena that support a post-materialist world-view include:

- The Abilities of Autistic Savants
- Terminal Lucidity
- The Shared-Death Experience
- Psychedelics
- The Placebo Effect
- Lucid Dreaming
- Precognition and Presentiment
- Clairvoyance/Remote Viewing
- Map Dowsing
- Telepathy

4

What Is the Consciousness Code?

It's trendy to call things "codes" these days. But broadly speaking, a code can be anything whose meaning, or very existence, is wholly or partly hidden or obscure. This may be deliberate, as with encrypted information. Or it may be a natural code, such as a DNA code, the shape of a plant's leaves, or the language of a particular bird species.

Some things may be hidden by possessing qualities that our senses are not physically equipped to perceive. Examples include radio waves, ultraviolet light, the air on a clear day, deep seismic rumbles, and ultrasonic dog whistles.

Other things in perfectly plain sight may be effectively invisible to us because our culture has no particular interest in them or is motivated to ignore or deny them. These can be difficult or impossible to recognize, and what we can't recognize we obviously can have no motivation to decode!

Consciousness is an excellent example of a code hiding in plain sight. On the one hand, nothing should be more immediate or obvious than our own consciousness. On the other, our materialistic culture puts enormous unspoken pressure on us to ignore it, or to explain it away as an illusory byproduct of neurological functioning. As a result, our chances of decoding it—laying bare its remarkable nature, proper-ties, and potentials—have tended to be slim.

So we end up like moviegoers, absorbed in a captivating adventure or love story while being oblivious to the screen, the projector, and the vast community of talented professionals behind the scenes. They don't exist in our reality unless we happen to be filmmakers or students of filmmaking who know what to look for and why to bother looking in the first place. Perhaps to make better movies?

As we have now seen, where honest science has stepped up to the plate and begun to decode and demystify consciousness, "better movies"—a richer appreciation of reality, more profound and beautiful experiences, and a healthier, more insightful relationship to life and death—appear to be an inevitable result. Coming soon to a realm near you!

People must appreciate that their picture of the material world is derived from and constructed solely on the basis of their own perception. There is simply no other way. All of us create our own reality on the basis of our consciousness. When we are in love the world is beautiful, and when we are depressed that very same world is a torment. In other words, the material "objective" world is merely a picture constructed in our own consciousness. People thus preserve their own worldview. This is precisely the kind of idea that a large part of the scientific community has difficulty accepting.

PIM VAN LOMMEL, M.D. AND
NDE RESEARCHER

Each of us creates our own reality. And if you disagree with me it proves my point.

NOMĒ, VEDANTA TEACHER

Chapter 4 Summary

- Codes, natural and artificial, exist all around us. Codes hiding in plain sight "don't exist" until we recognize them for what they are.
- Our own consciousness hides in plain sight. Becoming aware of it allows us to experience living and dying in a healthier, more comprehensive, beautiful, and masterful way.

5

Don't Eat the Menu!

Language gives us the illusion that we know, but we don't really know.

ECKHART TOLLE,
SPIRITUAL TEACHER AND AUTHOR

Language frames, structures, and colors our everyday picture of reality—including our deep-seated assumptions about life and death. It does so by providing the basic categories and associations whereby we construct our picture of the world. So when we speak to each other of everyday things our native tongue tends to serve us well enough. But when we poke our noses outside our culture's acknowledged spectrum of reality, language can become a trap, a mental prison, a misleading map, a thorny thicket, a hall of mirrors,* or even a nasty minefield.

Even our most familiar language is several steps removed from the realities to which it alludes. At best it's what Zen teachers call a "finger pointing at the moon," not the moon itself. Or a table of contents, not the book itself. Or a restaurant menu, not the food itself. So we need to

---

*Language is inherently meaningless. (If you don't believe me, try reading or listening to a language with which you're completely unfamiliar!) In the end it is we who give meaning to language, which then turns around and reflects back to us our individual and collective perceptions, norms, and prejudices.

take care not to confuse the symbol with the reality. We don't want to "eat the menu"!

Sadly, our modern Western languages have made it all but impossible to address the afterlife meaningfully. In our attempts to do so we're often mired in a confusing hodgepodge of traditional, popular, scientific, religious, invented, and repurposed terms. Some have been borrowed casually—sometimes awkwardly—from other languages and cultures, ancient and modern. English words like "heaven," "God," "divinity," "soul," and "spirit" can be laden with cultural baggage that can mean quite different things to different people. Judeo-Christians, Hindus, Buddhists, Muslims, New-Agers, secular humanists, curious scientists, and scowling skeptics may even come to blows over the meanings of such words! This is unhelpful. In the end, the better part of sanity may be to concede that we can't stuff a hundred pounds of reality into the five-pound bag of language and instead lean toward a less symbolic, more directly experiential grasp of the bigger picture.

> *Words reduce reality to something the human mind can grasp, which isn't very much.*
>
> ECKHART TOLLE,
> SPIRITUAL TEACHER AND AUTHOR

Meanwhile, let's at least see if we can find some clarity, have some fun, and hopefully clean up a few semantic messes by unpacking a few relevant words and phrases in our beloved bastard tongue known as modern English . . . in no particular order:

"Life"

Our culture, and therefore our language, says life is physical by definition. So any notion of "life after death" seems paradoxical, absurd, or downright impossible on its face. I mean, "life without life"? Come on. But what if life itself were one thing and its physical embodiments and expressions another? Hmmm . . .

Where the "Bodies" Are Buried

Where are the bodies buried? Well, some are buried right here in our English language. Consider words such as "everybody," "anybody," "somebody," and "nobody." With every repetition, don't these loaded words subtly reinforce the notion that we are nothing but our bodies?

Conversely, don't phrases like "kindly spirit" and "soul mate" send us a very different message about what a person might be in their essence?

At the very least, saying "everyone," "anyone," "someone," and so on helps shift our sense of identity from the body to the one who inhabits it.

The "Occult"

Eeeeek!!! Black Magic!! Well, not necessarily. "Occult" simply means "hidden" or "not obvious." For example, when one celestial body obscures or eclipses another, astronomers speak of "occultation." We tend to associate the term with the misuse of psychic powers, but that's mainly a way to sell admissions to horror movies and to scare people into joining religious institutions that would never themselves *dream* of messing with their devout adherents' psyches!

Granted, the misuse of power is often abetted by secrecy. But secrecy can also entertain, as with stage magic and movie magic, where revealing the inner workings of things would spoil all the awe, wonder, and fun!

"Mysticism"

In our popular culture the term is often dismissively equated with mystification, deliberate deception, or naive woo-woo. But in fact it simply means the pursuit of deep understanding through the sort of direct conscious experience that remains mysterious in the face of reductive analysis.

"Inner" vs. "Inner"

To those who equate the self exclusively with the physical body, "inner" can only mean the physical body's messy internal organs. But if the self is something beyond gross physiology, then the word "inner" points to our experience, to the complex subconscious aspects of our personalities, and ultimately to our observing awareness. Can you get more "inner" than that? I don't think so.

"Supernatural" and "Paranormal"

We often pigeonhole the afterlife, psychic abilities, and so forth as "supernatural." But who is to say that these things lie beyond the scope of nature? *We* do, by arbitrarily putting limits on the definition of "nature" that nature never asked for.

So if nature does include nonphysical realms of existence, then by definition they're perfectly natural, and no big deal.

But are they normal or *para*normal? Again, it is we who define these terms, based mainly on cultural conventions and norms, rather than actual understanding. For example, do we know with any certainty that our next-door neighbors don't have rollicking conversations with their dead aunts and uncles every Thursday at 9 p.m.? Let's admit that we don't, because our culture places strict limits on what's discussable. It polices this territory fearsomely and lays heavy penalties on those who venture outside its bounds.

So what's actually paranormal? Who knows?*

> *"Paranormal" and "supernatural" are just terms used to demarcate what academics are comfortable talking about in public.*
>
> DEAN RADIN, PH.D.

What about "Skepticism"?

Switch on your TV or surf the web, and sooner or later you'll be treated to the spectacle of "skeptics" being trotted out to aggressively

---

*To read a report on whether scientists and engineers report "exceptional human experiences" with the same frequency as the general population, see Wahbeh, et al., "Exceptional Experiences Reported by Scientists and Engineers."

debunk anything not canonized by today's mainstream sciences.

But wait a minute. To be properly skeptical simply means to question novel assertions and, in a spirit of curiosity, to carefully evaluate whatever evidence shows up in their favor. No more, no less.

Alas, in recent times skepticism has often escaped its proper place within the scientific method and metastasized into a cultish ideology that is fundamentally antithetical to the letter and spirit of science. This brand of "skepticism" is characterized less by careful evaluations of fact than by a naive belief in the finality of the real or imagined scientific status quo, primitive interpretations of "critical thinking," the thoughtless dismissal of unorthodox ideas prior to investigation, and, at its most extreme, personal attacks that can verge on slander. It is best thought of as *pseudo*skepticism.

One of pseudoskepticism's favorite ploys is to declare that something cannot possibly exist if we don't already understand its mechanism of action or have a theory that supports it in established terms. (On this basis alone science would grind to a halt, but never mind that.) Sadly, this mentality has spawned a self-appointed philosophical militia committed to the strict enforcement of mechanistic materialism as the state religion of science and academia.

One example of such intellectual militarism can be found in the pages of Wikipedia. Let me say for the record that I'm a great fan and frequent user of Wikipedia—but with one huge caveat: Wikipedia's unspoken editorial policies often embrace baseless, broad-brush, pseudoskeptical assertions about things and people considered to be outside the mainstream. In some cases individuals who claim to have been grievously maligned by Wikipedia's anonymous editors have been barred from correcting their own entries. Whether these practices rise to the level of defamation I will leave to those with applicable law degrees.

The brilliant website Skeptical about Skeptics includes nearly one hundred articles and essays on the scourge of pseudoskepticism, including my own lengthy satirical essay, "Zen . . . and the Art of Debunkery."

It also includes over a dozen articles that specifically address Wikipedia's dubious editorial practices.

> *There are two ways to be fooled. One is to believe what isn't true; the other is to refuse to believe what is true.*
>
> SØREN KIERKEGAARD, DANISH PHILOSOPHER

> *I shall not commit the fashionable stupidity of regarding everything I cannot explain as a fraud.*
>
> CARL JUNG, TWENTIETH-CENTURY PSYCHIATRIST
> AND PHILOSOPHER

You Want "Proof"?

So what's "proof"—of an afterlife or anything else? Unfortunately, what's considered "proven" can be as much a psychological and social question as anything else, in that typically it must conform to a consensus of current mainstream thought in any field. So theories and explanations that venture beyond the accepted paradigm are considered unproven *by definition*—at least until the paradigm shifts . . . or Hell freezes over.

So Why Do We Say "Afterlife"?

When we hear the word "afterlife," what springs to mind? Do we imagine a trivial appendage tacked on to the end of our "real" (physical) life, like the paper tail that blindfolded kids of my generation tried in vain to pin on paper donkeys at birthday parties? Or, at the other extreme, could the so-called afterlife be the main act, and our earthly life a temporary added attraction? Or could they be two sides of the same coin?

Ultimately each of us will have to answer these questions for ourselves—if not by dying, then at least by getting chummy with the related evidence and testimony.

In any case, why do we say "after"? One reason might be that we have received most of our information about the other side from those who have recently passed. So our culture finds it easier to think of our sojourn in the Greater Reality as *following* physical life rather than preceding it or bookending it. Up to a point, then, the term "afterlife" is understandable and forgivable, and, rather than lose too much sleep over it, we might as well concede the point. (Grumble.)

What's the "Veil"?

The "veil" is a popular metaphor for whatever separates "this world" from the "next world."

So is there a literal curtain or screen that blocks perception and communication between these worlds? If there is, the prime suspect appears to be our own physical senses, which are tuned to a very narrow slice of our natural environment. This thin slice then defines our everyday picture of reality.

> *Our [perceived reality] . . . is all that we know, and so we easily mistake it for all there is to know.*
>
> ED YONG, IN *AN IMMENSE WORLD*,
> EXPLORING THE MYSTERIES OF ANIMAL PERCEPTION

> *Human bodies are the fingers of blind souls.*
>
> DONALD JAMES HAMRICK, PHILOSOPHER, INVENTOR

Our limiting concepts, language, and social norms may contribute to the seeming opacity of the so-called veil, but surely our physical senses are its most stubbornly obvious constituent. As mentioned earlier, there are many demonstrably real things that they can't register with a ten-foot pole. Radio waves, ultrasonic sounds, infrared light, microorganisms, molecules, atoms, and subatomic phenomena swirl around us constantly but are effectively obscured by the bluntness and limited scope of our senses. Imagine listening to music through a filter that lets only two or three notes reach our ears. Or picture living in the midst of a beautiful landscape, locked inside a windowless cabin with nothing but a keyhole to peer out through. That's the general idea.

So when we arbitrarily limit "reality" to what our incarnated consciousness can perceive through the peephole of our physical senses, are we not capitulating to a sort of numbing hypnosis? On the other hand, when we open our minds and broaden our perceptions, do we not find that, lo and behold, there's more to behold? This becomes especially obvious when we put our blunt physical senses on hold through meditation, lucid dreaming, the use of mind-freeing plants and chemicals, and so forth.

Pseudoskeptics love to deny the existence of "invisible realities." How easily they forget that science has been exploring them for centuries, by devising instruments that allow us to bring previously "nonexistent" phenomena into our narrow sensory spectrum. While these instruments haven't actually broadened the scope of our physical senses, they do send us some important and powerful messages: to open our minds, ask questions, start noticing clues, and acknowledge that what we habitually perceive is not all there is to perceive.

> *Our normal waking consciousness . . . is but one special type of consciousness, whilst all about it, parted from it by the filmiest of screens, there lie potential forms of consciousness entirely different. . . . No account of the universe in its totality can be final which leaves these other forms of consciousness quite disregarded.*
>
> WILLIAM JAMES, NINETEENTH-CENTURY
> AMERICAN PHILOSOPHER

"Imagination"

I imagine we've all heard the dismissive phrase, "Oh, it's *only* a figment of your imagination!"

But let's look around us and realize that every single product of human design and manufacture, and every work of art, literature, and music, began as a figment of someone's imagination. Not too shabby, is it?

Our imagination consciously or unconsciously serves us almost every moment of our life, in setting our immediate and long-term goals, giving form to our needs and desires, zeroing in on solutions to problems, and choreographing our dreams.

As we'll see, befriending and mastering this priceless, powerful, *very real* tool is as much a key to a good afterlife as it is to a fulfilling, productive, and creative embodied life.

OK, so What about "God"?

Depending on whom you ask, the English word "God" can mean:

- The popular Judeo-Christian patriarch: a grandfatherly white-bearded white male cloaked in white, surrounded by winged white cherubs, floating on puffy white clouds. He creates universes with a word and dispenses lightning bolts, catastrophic floods, blessings, and forgiveness in equal measure. This seems to be the definition most beloved by atheists, who proudly point out the absence of evidence for such a being outside of Renaissance paintings and New Yorker cartoons.
- The Great Unknown—a nebulous catchall for everything beyond our current understanding.
- The collective consciousness of the entire universe.
- The consciousness that *created* the collective consciousness of the entire universe.

Enough.

If "God" means anything at all, it seems to mean whatever might be the undivided source or substrate of all things and all awareness in all dimensions of reality. I suppose we can live with that definition or something like it.

You may disagree.

God, in Hebrew, is "Elohim," or, slightly later—just before the time of Jesus—"Elo-ha." Aramaic changes it to "Alla-ha." Arabic changes it to "Allah." None of it actually means "God," although Muslims, Christians and Jews will argue with you endlessly about this. But "God" is the placeholder for that which is the mystery—the Reality of all.

NEIL DOUGLAS-KLOTZ,
RELIGIOUS SCHOLAR AND AUTHOR

Since no one really knows anything about God, those who think they do are just troublemakers.

ATTRIBUTED TO RABIA OF BASRA,
THE FIRST FEMALE SUFI SAINT

Who's an "Atheist"?

Spoiler alert: I consider myself an atheist. Does that sound odd, coming from an afterlife researcher? Not really. To most modern folks of my acquaintance, atheism means a disbelief in some version of that floating Caucasian patriarch. I happen to share that disbelief.

So when asked, I reply, "I'm an atheist, but I'm not a materialist."

So How about "Objective Truth"?

Does objective truth exist? I can't give you an objective answer, but personally I doubt it because what passes for objectivity often turns out be a human consensus—one that can be fragile and fleeting. At best, objectivity is a moving target.

Can we know and describe even a simple, common object objectively? To find out, let's fire up our imaginations and do a little thought experiment, starting with a table. Surely most living and working spaces on most inhabited planets have at least one. So why don't we sit down at a typical one—say, a simple, square one with four legs—and check it out?

If we're artists or industrial designers, we may notice only the table's particular aesthetics and structure.

If we're furniture makers, we may notice only the table's physical dimensions, how it was built, and what it was made of.

If we're chemists, we may wonder only about the glue that fastens the veneer to the tabletop.

If we're janitors, we may consider only how easy it might be to move when we clean up at the end of the day.

If we're writers, waiters, philosophers, gamblers, or accountants, we aren't likely to notice much about it at all, except to the extent that it serves our practical needs.

If we're materialist pseudoskeptics, we'll pound our fist on it mercilessly and declare, "THIS IS REALITY!!" without giving the poor table itself much consideration.

If we're physicists, we may view it as 99.99999 percent empty space.

So is that table described objectively by any one of those observers? Or by the sum total of their observations? Only in a very limited sense, because we can never know how many more observations might be made of that table and from how many different points of view.

Hey! We've just noticed that it's a nice, sunny afternoon, so let's get up from our imaginary table and go outside for an imaginary walk. Soon an airplane passes overhead, but if we're like most folks, that plane "doesn't exist," in that we take no notice of it at all. But to a bunch of pilots and aviation buffs strolling along the way, not only will it immediately exist but they may correctly identify its type, its vintage, and even its country of origin just by its particular sound.

Meanwhile, our imaginary aviation buffs completely fail to notice a species of flower growing by the wayside, which some imaginary botanists walking a distance behind them automatically notice and identify in an eyeblink.

Now, to conclude our imaginary walk, let's stroll alongside a road we had *only* driven countless times over the years. And suddenly we notice something: "OMG! Was THAT there all this time?"

Have we stepped into a parallel universe? Probably not. Instead we've just learned that what passes for objective truth is at best selective and tentative. This is confirmed over and over again, each time the "definitive" conclusions of "objective" science are rendered obsolete by new information, observations, and understandings acquired through the scientific method itself.*

Finally, let's concede that the simple metaphors and examples given above don't begin to include all the complex blind spots, biases, institutional demands, and peer pressures that opinionated humans inevitably bring to virtually every real-life situation.

So much for "objective truth."

> *Whoever undertakes to set himself up as a judge of Truth
> and Knowledge is shipwrecked by the laughter of the gods.*
>
> ALBERT EINSTEIN

"Form" vs. "Essence"

Understanding the difference between "form" and "essence" is one of the keys to grasping the notion of an afterlife, in which one's essence endures despite one's abandonment of a particular physical form.

The *form* of anything is, of course, its physical makeup and outer appearance. Its *essence* is the seemingly intangible core of its identity. Essence is the life of things—an enduring, invulnerable, unique *beingness* that may prefer a particular physical expression or embodiment but isn't dependent on it.

"Mind"

This one's hard to nail down because it's such a catchall word. Google Translate lists 52 English synonyms for "mind." Its French translation lists 108!

---

*Until 1925 we believed that our own Milky Way galaxy constituted the entire universe. As of 2021 the estimates of the number of galaxies in the universe ran somewhere between two hundred million and two trillion. (Oops! As of 2022, the James Webb Space Telescope has just blown those estimates out of the water and once again threatened to throw our dominant cosmological theories into disarray.)

Depending on the context, "mind" can mean consciousness or awareness itself. "*The* mind" can mean one's capacity for forming particular thoughts, imagination, mental skills, and so forth. It is also a verb with multiple meanings and nuances.

Geeky folks with an emotional bias toward hyperintellectual, left-brained functioning tend to equate the mind with analytical thinking and with the sort of computational intelligence that can be produced artificially.

Creatives tend to identify it more with the open-ended, imaginative activity associated with the right hemisphere of the brain.

I tend to think of the mind as a "weaver of the threads of consciousness."

Spiritual teachers often view the mind as a sort of mischievous faculty—a runaway machine that endlessly (mindlessly?!) pumps out ideas, images, associations, trains of thought, and so forth, which can distract us from connecting with the simple fact of our own awareness.

"Spirit" vs. "Consciousness"

They tend to mean the same thing. I prefer "consciousness" because it's more neutral and seems to carry less cultural baggage.

But "spirit" does have its place in many contexts as an intangible quality or feeling; i.e., a spirit of enthusiasm, love, humor, and so forth. Spirit isn't a *thing*.

In casual speech, "*a* spirit" can also mean a disembodied or quasi-physical entity, such as a ghost or a wispy apparition. And let's not forget that beverages made mainly of alcohol, which evaporates invisibly into thin air, are also known as "spirits." Cheers!

"Consciousness"

So what is consciousness? No, it isn't a thing. But if we absolutely must come up with a more-or-less tangible picture of it, we might think of it roughly as a light, flowing substance or field of energy. It extends infinitely and has no particular shape or form. Like paint or a sculptor's batch of raw clay, its forms depend on how it is influenced by what shapes it—in this case, its own observations, feelings, motives, intentions, memories, inspiration, knowledge, creative imagination, and perhaps myriad influences for which we have no language. It is infinitely expandable and malleable—so completely unlike the delimited, structured, "hard-coded" nature of the physical universe that it's ridiculously difficult to grasp conceptually. But it's ridiculously easy to experience directly: Just imagine an elephant in a pink tutu, and . . . *poof!* An image of an elephant in a pink tutu appears out of nowhere, dancing daintily.* Consciousness is magic!

Now, if, as we increasingly suspect, consciousness is indeed fundamental or primary, one might think of it as the "ultimate substance," or as some term it the "ultimate ground of being."

As the ultimate creator and decider, it alone would be responsible for its creations and decisions—it would be unable to pass the buck of causality to some other real or imagined agency, mechanism, or scapegoat. It couldn't honestly claim "The devil made me do it!"

Primary, fundamental, or ultimate—take your pick—would mean that consciousness simply IS. If that's the case, then by definition it's not reducible to anything else. Attempts to dissect or analyze it to find out what makes it tick will meet with disappointment, because *nothing makes it tick. It just ticks.* That's its nature.

Wait. What's that sound . . . ?

Ah! It's a choir of materialists shouting from the housetops in five-part harmony: "Cop-out! Everything in the universe must be made of parts that are made of smaller parts that are made of particles that are reducible to smaller particles . . . and so on!"

---

*Those who suffer from the rare condition known as "aphantasia" or mental blindness are unable to perceive mental pictures. Conversely, some individuals can apparently see their physical environment psychically. Several books offer training in this discipline, known as "mind sight." See the entries under Hopkins and also McNamara in the recommended reading list.

Great fleas have little fleas upon their backs to bite 'em,
And little fleas have lesser fleas, and so ad infinitum.

AUGUSTUS DE MORGAN,
NINETEENTH-CENTURY BRITISH MATHEMATICIAN

But over the entire course of history, no particles of consciousness have ever shown up.

We may *associate* consciousness with dissectable things like brains and their patterns of functioning, because consciousness can work through brains and be affected by them, just as sunlight can be affected by passing through stained glass. But a physical brain is no more equivalent to consciousness than a radio receiver is equivalent to music, or a stained glass window can be equated with sunlight, or an automobile equals the enjoyment of a journey.

No actual experience—no sight, sound, smell, taste, feeling, thought, or intuition—has ever been found by dissecting a brain or analyzing its activity. Nor could it be, because experience is subjective *by definition*. Sure, we can label certain activities, like surfing, skydiving, bowling, or knitting, "experiences," but that's no more than a convention of language that reflects our culture's externalist bias.

"Soul"

A "soul" is usually thought of as something more individualized or self-contained than raw "spirit" or "consciousness at large." "Soul" implies a particular identity with boundaries of some kind. If consciousness is like a limitless ocean, a soul might be likened to a surfer's wave, albeit one that endures over time.

"Soul groups" or "group souls" in the afterlife are said to be like peas in a pod or leaves on a tree branch—souls that participate in a more comprehensive whole that has its own identity at a higher level but which retains and respects the unique individuality of the smaller entities it contains.

"Separation" vs. "Distinction"

Is a wave *separate* from the ocean or only *distinct?* In other words, if the ultimate ground of being is consciousness, is our individualized soul actually separate from that ground, or is it, like that surfer's wave, merely a distinctive region of the same stuff? This isn't mere semantic hairsplitting; it looms as a central issue in our understanding of the nature of individuality in physical life and in the afterlife.

Sleep on this question and see where it takes you.

The Big Semantic Kahuna: "Reality"!

Our materialistic Western culture is accustomed to thinking of reality as the sum total of the building blocks of the physical universe that are so meticulously cataloged by our physical sciences. So naturally, anything that suggests a coexisting or more comprehensive definition of reality seems like an impossibility or maybe a joke.

But let's set the vastness of the universe aside for a moment. In everyday matters, what does any one of us really mean by "reality"?

Ask any two individuals about politics, food, or fashion and they'll tell you what's *really* best and *really* real, each from their own point of view. Each will preface their opinions by saying "actually" and "but really," to convince you of the absoluteness of their take on reality. But since neither of their realities can wholly line up with the other's (see "objective truth," p. 50), we won't find any ultimate enlightenment there.

Ah, but science must have the definitive answers! After all, its methods rely on hard, quantifiable evidence and time-tested procedures, which is more than one can say for fashion or politics.

This may be true in theory, but in practice the sciences are pursued by—drumroll, please—scientists! As human beings, scientists make their own individual and collective choices about what subject matter to study, how to prioritize it, what evidence to include or exclude, what methods to employ, where to publish their results, whose critiques to accept, how to allocate their budgets to please their funding sources, and so forth. So naturally these choices are not always made on a purely rational basis, but often to keep families fed and reputations polished by following the unspoken rules of one's professional and academic communities. Want to keep your research funds, teaching job, or tenure? Great. Just don't shine the light of science into, ahem, certain areas, and nobody will get hurt.*

> *In theory, theory and practice are the same. In practice, they're not.*
>
> YOGI BERRA, BASEBALL PLAYER AND
> FOLK PHILOSOPHER

> *Most scientists trust what they hear from others. And so if they're hearing from others that there's nothing to this evidence, then they don't go to look at it.*
>
> DIANE HENNACY POWELL, M.D.

So while the scientific method may be valid and reliable where it applies, and when it can be followed without undue bias or outright misconduct,† many of its vaunted declarations should probably be viewed as "the best we can do for now under the circumstances."

To expect science to yield the Absolute Truth about reality in some religious or ideological fashion will sooner or later end in grief. *Why?* Well, apart from the above considerations, science perpetually evolves, not only in its details but in its basic paradigms—its very "frameworks of understanding."

---

*Ever heard of John E. Mack? Look him up on Wikipedia and scroll down to "Investigation by Harvard." Then read Ralph Blumenthal's biography *The Believer*.

†If you're unfamiliar with scientific misconduct, Wikipedia offers a good starting point. Also see Else and Van Noorden, "The Fight Against Fake-Paper Factories That Churn Out Sham Science."

A wonderful example, once again, is contemporary astronomy, in which strongly held theories are questioned, abandoned, and superseded year upon year, as our increasingly sophisticated instruments, practices, and concepts reveal how much we still don't understand, even about the physical universe.

This uncertainty is expressed perfectly in an anecdote about Albert Einstein, when he was teaching at a university. A student came up to him and asked, "Is it true that the final exam this year has the same questions as last year?" Einstein replied, "Yes, but the answers have changed!"

So where does this leave us in our attempt to define "reality"?

Square one. So what to do?

OK. If we must have such a slippery word in our language at all, maybe we can settle on a reasonable *working* definition. How about this one? Reality is *whatever can give rise to consequences.*

If we can accept this for the sake of discussion, we can safely say that *everything* is real, since anything physical, mental, emotional, or spiritual can lead to consequences—if not in the physical world, then in the world of our experience. Viewed this way, even distorted facts and outright lies are demonstrably real: ask any judge, journalist, or repentant who must grapple with their consequences and implications daily. By this same standard, dreams, the flavor of chocolate ice cream, and everything else of which we have knowledge or experience—is *real.*

How about knowledge and experience themselves? Yup. Real. For sure.

How about things whose mechanism of action is not yet understood? Affirmative. Even their mechanism of action is real.

What about everything else that remains to be discovered? Real.

This definition of reality also ushers us into the realm of creativity—the arts, literature, poetry, and so on—which draw inspiration from myriad inner and outer influences and include open-ended possibilities.

Where else can such a definition take us?

One place is the perspective of indigenous and shamanic cultures, whose take on reality appears to be more comprehensive and less filtered, fragmented, sliced and diced than ours. Many of these cultures employ *verb*-centric languages, which presuppose a radically different sense of reality than is implied by our *noun*-centric ones.

If these aren't enough to open our minds to the nonphysical aspects of reality, let's not forget the utterly abstract realms of mathematics, pure information, and music. While these may be expressed or embodied physically, their essence is independent of any particular embodiment. Yet surely no one would dismiss them as unreal.

> *Do not cry for me, for I go where music comes from.*
>
> ATTRIBUTED TO JOHANN SEBASTIAN BACH
> ON HIS DEATHBED

Finally, let's not forget that even in the realm of conventional physics, forces and fields (i.e., gravity and magnetism, as well as electric and electromagnetic fields) play essential roles. Though utterly immaterial, they are undeniably real.

So, to the bottom line: Are the infinite worlds of consciousness more or less real than the finite, physical world? Perhaps the most meaningful answer might be, "It depends on where your attention is focused at any given moment."

"Time"

Is time real, too? Since it can give rise to consequences I suppose it is, though the word has at least two very different meanings.

Physical time is based on the rate at which things change, move, orbit, vibrate, or oscillate (tick, tock, tick, tock) in the physical domain. Because this rate is consistent enough everywhere in our world we can build clocks that allow us to synchronize and synergize our activities. This sense of stability and predictability may be one of the reasons why we tend to focus our sense of reality outside of us.

Subjective time is based on the perceived rate at which our individual experience unfolds within our awareness. It goes slowly when we're bored or hungry (*"When will that damn waiter get here with our food?!"*) and it flies when we're having fun (*"Sigh . . . I could do this forever, but Dad gets home in fifteen minutes!"*) or getting older (*"Where the hell's the time going?!"*). And of course in dreams—in which hours of subjective time can be experienced in minutes of physical time—all bets are off.*

But instead of granting each kind of time its own validity, we tend to regard physical time as the "gold standard" and subjective time as an orphan child or illusory bugaboo.

So what happens at death, when our inner experience is uncoupled from the ticktock time of the physical domain? Anyone who's ever experienced dreaming can answer that in a flash: though we may still experience a linear sequence of events, the flow of time becomes flexible and elastic. But wait a minute. We've already established that it's elastic even in the midst of life! Subjective time is *always* with us, regardless of outer circumstances.

So could subjective time be the "gold standard"?

If so, what are the limits of its elasticity? Can we even experience absolute timelessness? Having had this experience personally, I can answer in the affirmative. It felt like pure, infinite, eternal awareness. No beginning. No end. The main takeaway? The realization that *eternity is not merely an infinite extension of time. It's something utterly and completely different. Wow!*

---

*Some dream experiences even include remembered pasts or histories. For example, in a dream I had some years ago, I walked past the home of a particular woman with whom I recalled, in some detail, having had a lengthy partnership. I awoke from this dream quite astonished, since no such person had existed in my waking life.

"Space"

As with time, space can be either physical or subjective.

Physical space is measurable by agreed-upon standards—inches, feet, meters, miles, light-years, and so on—arranged in three mutually exclusive dimensions.

Our subjective sense of space is reckoned by individual inner experience. For example, what seems comfortably spacious or annoyingly crowded can depend on the physical size of one's own body—airplane seating springs to mind! But our spatial sense is also influenced by cultural norms and personal taste: Is an apartment or a mansion adequate to our comfort and satisfaction? Our individual sense of physical space may also differ for emotional, psychological, neurological, or physiological reasons including spatial and depth perception. (For some folks, parallel parking is at best a struggle steeped in mystery and fraught with incalculable risk!) Interior designers know that a mirror wall can double the experienced size of a physically small room. And of course, in dreams, subjective space can be a mind-pretzeling, labyrinthine crapshoot, yet within the dream we accept it as naturally as our waking self accepts physical space. How interesting is that?

"Incarnation"

Incarnation can be thought of as a magnetic embrace of mind and matter. More mundanely, it's like climbing into the driver's seat of a car: suddenly our sense of self merges with the car and we relate to the world as if we are a car among other cars. (*"Damn! He hit me in the right rear fender!!"*) Inside the car our body's repertoire of movements has now been reduced to just a few puny ones—we can no longer walk, run, dance, jump, swim, or do cartwheels. But we now have particular powers, abilities, and opportunities that our body doesn't have on its own. Similarly, when we incarnate, we trade off a certain freedom, flexibility, and spaciousness against a more highly focused and tightly structured mode of being.

Incarnation is said to be an experiment in consciousness that places our earthly identity at the midway or balance point between infinite awareness and finite matter. It shoehorns our expansive sense of identity and our unique trove of inner faculties* into a physical package that provides us with a special point of presence within the vast landscape of physical nature. This includes a set of biological, cultural, and social boundaries that distinguish us from the rest of creation—a unique personal identity with all the trimmings. It enables us to acquire particular knowledge, skills, and experiences in a focused way, to conduct our lives as works of art, and to take these treasures with us when we exit our worn-out or damaged vehicles (bodies) and make our way back into the infinite dimensions, shared realities, and freedom of the afterlife.

> *You are an aperture through which the universe is looking at and exploring itself.*
>
> ALAN WATTS, PHILOSOPHER, WRITER

"Death"

From a collective point of view, death appears to be an indispensable feature of life. After all, without the turnover of the physical bodies of plants, animals, and people, our planet would long ago have choked on its own reproductive abundance.

So death keeps things balanced and in harmony.

This year's food crop dies, recycling nutrients and making space for the next year's crop to grow.

---

*Our human self obviously incorporates and integrates multiple levels and faculties of perception, thought, experience, and behavior—"sub-selves" that can function quasi-independently. After all, we can walk and chew gum at the same time, while observing and appreciating our surroundings, listening to music (or hearing it—or even composing it!—in our heads), heeding street signs, scratching an itch, and worrying about our finances. We can drive while daydreaming, whistling a tune, and listening to the latest ghastly newscast and usually get to our destination safely. Can a robot do all that? I don't think so.

Generations of humans come and go. As their bodies and brains age and their minds grow feeble or set in their ways, death overtakes them, cleansing the physical and mental environment and making way for new generations to arrive, thrive, love, be challenged, laugh, cry, and learn the intricacies of life in a physical universe.

> *A new scientific truth does not triumph by convincing its opponents and making them see the light, but rather because its opponents eventually die, and a new generation grows up that is familiar with it.*
>
> PHYSICIST MAX PLANCK

This is all well and good collectively, but what about the individual experience of death? It's no secret that the dying process (which we also confusingly call "death") can often be fraught with physical pain, distress, doubts, fears, confusion, and heartbreak. But once the cord is cut and we've shed our old skin, what remains of us? Where do we go, and why? Is death on this side like birth on the other side? Is it, as some have claimed, like a homecoming of sorts?

We'll explore these questions in part three of this book.

Meanwhile let's take a fascinating detour through some of the most stubbornly incontrovertible evidence for a continued existence beyond the threshold of physical death.

> *Science appears to preclude the existence of an afterlife. But science evolves, and there's no knowing what possibilities might be acceptable to a future science.*
>
> BRIAN JOSEPHSON, PH.D., physicist, NOBEL LAUREATE

Chapter 5 Summary

- Language only points to things and shouldn't be confused with the things themselves.
- Our language reflects back to us our own cultural norms and presuppositions.
- Post-materialist thinking invites us to take a fresh look at language, how it influences what we take to be reality, and what possibilities it forbids or permits us to consider.

PART II

Some of the Best Evidence for the Continuity of Consciousness

Introduction to Part II

In 2003 coproducer Tim Coleman and I embarked on the production of a documentary film series that would seek out and explore the most compelling evidence for an afterlife. Our travels took us across the United States and to four European countries. The outcome was a pair of documentaries representing what, in our view, comprised the two most outstanding bodies of evidence supporting the existence of an afterlife and the reality of communication between our physical world and the Greater Reality.

Chapter 6 is based on our ninety-five-minute feature documentary, *Calling Earth*, which examines the mind-boggling field of Instrumental Trans-Communication (ITC)—communication from the other side through modern electronics—and documents many examples of these phenomena. In my view ITC is far and away the most convincing and accessible example of consciousness functioning within a nonphysical matrix. After you've read chapter 6, I encourage you to see the film for free at bit.ly/callearth. There's a five-minute preview at bit.ly/callearth-preview.

Chapter 7 is based on our eighty-five-minute feature documentary, *Scole: The Afterlife Experiment,* which examines what I believe to be the most robustly evidential experiment ever conducted in the realm of physical mediumship. You can see it for free at bit.ly/scolemovie.

In chapter 8 you'll meet a young American boy, James Leininger, who, practically from birth, was deeply impacted by visceral memories of having been a young American pilot who was shot down by the Japanese during World War II. The Leininger case is one of the most robustly documented and widely reported reincarnation cases of modern times.

6

Electronic Communications from the Other Side

Mysterious Voices on Tape

One of the defining characteristics of the post-World-War-II era—the late 1940s and '50s—was the conversion of wartime industries to the production and marketing of modern consumer goods: cars that magically shifted their own gears, microwave ovens that nuked frozen food in a flash, and a TV set or two in every home.

A concurrent innovation was the audio tape recorder. This nifty device enabled radio personalities, musicians, birthday celebrants, and Sunday preachers to immortalize their priceless music and words of wisdom on reels of cheap, reusable, magnetically coated plastic tape.

Some of these early recorders had an annoying habit of picking up stray signals from powerful radio stations located nearby. So when spurious voices were occasionally heard on recorded tapes, they were initially dismissed as pesky instances of "radio pickup."

But were all these voices in fact nothing but random bits of radio programs?

Friedrich Juergenson's Nocturnal Adventure

Late one evening in 1959, prominent Swedish artist and filmmaker Friedrich Juergenson was using his new recorder to tape nocturnal bird sounds for a documentary. When he played back the tape he was dismayed to find his recording spoiled by an annoying case of what he assumed was radio pickup. But strangely, these faint voices seemed to be *discussing* nocturnal bird sounds! Quite a coincidence, he thought. Shortly thereafter, another faint voice on his tapes sounded uncannily like his own deceased mother calling him by his childhood nickname, "Friedel." At that point Juergenson threw up his hands and had to admit that something quite extraordinary was going on. Whatever it was, it begged to be studied scientifically.

So Juergenson began to experiment. He would roll the tape, record a question, wait a few moments, ask another question, and so on. On playback, in the gaps where there should have been only silence, he heard faint but appropriate responses to his questions. This launched Juergenson's lifelong quest to explore what is now known as the Electronic Voice Phenomenon, or EVP.

Konstantin Raudive's Experiments

Juergenson was soon approached by a Latvian psychologist and professor, Konstantin Raudive (RAOW-dee-vuh), who worked with Juergenson for a time and then proceeded to conduct his own EVP experiments. Raudive went on to record, by some accounts, as many as 70,000 anomalous voices in six languages. In 1971 he published a phonograph record titled *Breakthrough,* which included dozens of these voices responding to his questions. His German book on the subject, *Unhörbares Wird Hörbar* (the inaudible becomes audible), was also released in English as *Breakthrough.*

Raudive passed on in 1974, but during the 1980s and '90s he gained a reputation as the undisputed champion among electronic afterlife communicators. During that period—a sort of golden age of EVP—experimenters on at least three continents were hearing and recording Raudive's voice via telephone, radio, and directly on recording tapes. Raudive spoke a half-dozen languages fluently, with German and English most prominent in these communications. While most examples of EVP last only a few moments and can vary in their clarity, Raudive has been able to sustain clear, robust conversations lasting several minutes. His voice, character, accent, and warm-but-gruff personality have remained consistent and clearly identifiable across all recordings in all media on several continents.

One day in January 1994, writer and EVP experimenter Mark Macy, of Boulder, Colorado, heard his phone ring, picked up the receiver, and was astonished to hear the voice of Raudive offering some technical advice for a radio EVP experiment Macy was conducting at the time. Macy had no way of recording the call, but he soon installed recording equipment on his phone line and was prepared when Raudive rang again. Here is part of the ensuing dialogue:

I'll try to make it clearer this time. It's a VLF receiving converter. You simply connect the converter to your HF radio's antenna input and a suitable VLF antenna. Then you convert the entire VLF band—let's say 10 kilohertz to 500 kilohertz—up to 4,010 to 4,500 kilohertz respectively. Technical advice from this side.

Raudive's advice was impeccable, but it wasn't limited to technical matters; he also addressed social issues, such as drugs and violence, as these are viewed—apparently with great concern—by those on the other side.

Sarah Estep and the AAEVP

Sarah Estep was an American EVP pioneer who made hundreds of her own EVP recordings. Estep founded the first organization to promote the research and practice of EVP, the American Association for Electronic Voice Phenomena (AAEVP). Since her passing in 2008 the organization, now known as Association Transcommunication, has been ably led by retired communications engineer Tom Butler and psychologist Lisa Butler.

Ernst Senkowski

German physicist Ernst Senkowski (1922–2015), a former UNESCO physics expert, was another pioneering ITC researcher. He coined the term Instrumental Trans-Communication and published dozens of papers and books on the subject in German and English. His book *Instrumental Transcommunication* is regarded as the most influential publication in the field.

Grass-Roots EVP

Following the pioneering experimenters noted above, ordinary folks eventually joined the ranks of these practitioners. They've achieved success using simple cassette tape recorders, digital memo recorders, personal computers, and smartphone recording apps. One example is the Big Circle, a group of American mothers who have maintained electronic communications with their deceased children—in some cases for decades (see p. 110).

Direct Radio Voice

Direct Radio Voice (DRV) is a phenomenon in which communications from the deceased are heard on radio receivers that are tuned to blank spaces between broadcast stations.

Notable DRV researcher-practitioners include Anabela Cardoso, a former Portuguese diplomat who now resides in the Galicia region of Spain. Cardoso has organized international conferences devoted to the development of electronic afterlife communications, has published a regular journal on the subject, and is the author of several books, including *Electronic Voices, Electronic Contact with the Dead*, and *Glimpses of Another World*. She has also produced a series of videos that can be seen on YouTube.

By far the most remarkable DRV practitioner of all was Marcello Bacci of Grosseto, Italy. From the early 1970s until his retirement in 2019, Bacci conducted hundreds of public sessions in which his old vacuum-tube radio receiver faithfully emitted the voices of countless deceased individuals, permitting their relatives to experience two-way conversations with their loved ones on the other side. Over the years Bacci never charged a penny for his services, and skeptical forensics failed to reveal hoaxing of any kind.

From EVP to ITC

In the early years of electronic afterlife communication the audio connection expanded into text and images that were received on early home computers with no internet connection. Images of the deceased also appeared on television screens, in film and digital cameras, and in faxes. EVP had now evolved into the broader field of Instrumental Trans-Communication (ITC).

Computer Messages from the Other Side

During the 1990s and early 2000s, experimenter Mark Macy worked with an international network of ITC researchers, including a group in the small European country of Luxembourg. In October 1995 this group sent Macy a message in text form that had apparently shown up on their computer. In this message, an obscure, deceased journalist, Arthur Beckwith, claimed he was born in Sunderland, England in 1832, migrated to Jamaica and eventually New York City, became a reporter for a major Brooklyn newspaper, and died in 1912. Macy's subsequent research on two continents confirmed every detail of Beckwith's life exactly as claimed in his message.

A claimed instance of anomalous computer messaging showed up in my own life some years ago after I had hired a young woman as a film-production assistant. Over lunch one day she seemed agitated and a bit teary-eyed so I asked her what was up.

"You won't believe me."

I said, "Try me."

"Promise not to tell anyone?"

I promised.

"Yesterday I . . . uh . . . received an email from my dead uncle."

I must have smiled slightly upon hearing this or perhaps raised my eyebrows because she said, "See, I told you you wouldn't believe me."

I said, "Actually, I've heard of that sort of thing and I'm fascinated. Please tell me more."

"Well, I was raised in an abusive family, and my uncle had sort of been my protector. He worked for Shell Oil, and they eventually transferred him to their Singapore office. Then, not too long ago, he passed away.

"Yesterday, out of nowhere, this email simply appeared on my computer's desktop, with a message of love from my uncle. The sender's address was 'singapore at yahoo.com.' I tried replying, but [at that time] there was no such address and the reply bounced.

"Oh, and one other thing. Attached to the email there was a photo of me and my boyfriend, which had been taken by some friends last week when we were visiting Colorado. The people we were with knew nothing of my uncle."

Visual ITC

Friedrich Juergenson predicted that images of the deceased would eventually appear on television screens. Juergenson spent his later years in southern Sweden and died in 1987. At the moment of his burial, his friends Claude and Ellen Thorlin, who lived 250 miles to the north near Stockholm, felt compelled to switch on their TV and tune it to an unused channel. Having done so, they were astonished to witness an unmistakable likeness of Juergenson appearing on its screen, which they captured in a Polaroid photograph.

Earlier, Klaus Schreiber, of Aachen, Germany, had succeeded in capturing images of deceased relatives and several notable individuals on an early home videotape system. After Schreiber himself passed in 1988, his likeness was said to have appeared spontaneously on the personal computer operated by the Luxembourg group, which they claimed was not connected to any outside network. Later, German physicist Ernst Senkowski recorded a lengthy telephone call from Schreiber, which included personal greetings to various colleagues and a highly evidential message relayed from Senkowski's own deceased father.

Robbert van den Broeke of the Netherlands* has, for decades, been producing a stunning variety of anomalous images in film and digital cameras handed to him by visitors, scientists, and journalists. These often include the likenesses of deceased persons. In 2014 I visited Robbert for a week and established stringent protocols to eliminate any possibility of deception. Under these conditions, he produced four remarkable images, two of which appeared to resemble EVP pioneer Friedrich Juergenson in his later years.

> *What my research has convinced me is that there is another dimension to our existence. And that includes life after death.*
>
> ALEXANDER MACRAE, EVP EXPERIMENTER,
> ELECTRONICS ENGINEER, DEVELOPER OF
> SPEECH ENHANCERS FOR NASA'S SPACE SHUTTLE

Chapter 6 Summary

- Voices and images of deceased individuals have appeared in analog and digital sound-recording and imaging systems for at least seventy years.
- Digital text and faxes from the other side have been received for at least forty years.
- These phenomena have been objects of ongoing research and refinement, and are used by some as a practical means of connecting with departed loved ones.
- You can review these cases, get more detail, and see images and much more in my documentary, *Calling Earth* at bit.ly/callearth.

---

*You can find a good overview of Robbert's talents in "Introduction to the Robbert van den Broeke Case" by Nancy Talbott on the BLT Research Team's website.

7

The Scole Experiment

The tiny hamlet of Scole is nestled in the English countryside, in the county of Norfolk, about a half hour's drive northeast of Cambridge. You can walk through its historic central district in a minute or two. Driving through you might almost miss it, but for a heraldic sign that dominates its tiny central park. Its main street is named "The Street." Tucked behind the Scole Inn, founded in 1655, is the Street Farmhouse, which also dates from the seventeenth century. In its quiet brick cellar, between 1994 and 1999, a small group of experimenters conducted the longest-running, most successful experiment in physical mediumship ever attempted.

What Is Physical Mediumship?

Physical mediumship seeks to create conditions whereby those on the other side can interact directly with the physical world, producing phenomena that can be perceived by our ordinary senses, and be collected, preserved, or recorded for later study and analysis. It is usually accomplished through sustained, focused intention, meditative states, a conducive environment, and apparent cooperation from entities on the other side. The practice has had a long and controversial history—sadly, including some trickery and fraud. But just as scientific misconduct hardly represents the whole of science, deceptive behavior has little to do with sincere, well-organized efforts to interact with the consciousness of those who inhabit the Greater Reality.

The Scole Experiment is one of the finest examples of such efforts, having been confirmed as genuine by numerous independent observers and credentialed scientists. The experiment was openly reported in the press, became the subject of two books and a three-hundred-page scientific report, and was the focus of the feature documentary *Scole: The Afterlife Experiment,* on which this chapter is based.

What Was the Scole Experiment and What Did It Accomplish?

The Scole Experiment was conducted principally by two couples. Investigators Robin and Sandra Foy had spent more than half a lifetime studying and writing about physical mediumship. Rounding out the four-member "Scole Group" were two of Britain's most accomplished mental mediums, Diana and Alan Bennett.

Their colleagues on the other side communicated verbally through the Bennetts, in accents ranging from British to North American, Irish, and East Indian. This otherworldly "Spirit Team" was said to have been organized and conducted by a deceased Victorian lady, Mrs. Emily Bradshaw. The Team itself comprised a group of talented souls, most of whom claimed to have lived in the British Isles, Europe, North America, or India during the nineteenth and early twentieth centuries. Some identified themselves as poets, artists, and photographers, others as philosophers, scientists, and engineers. Some possessed particular talents, such as the ability to project their voices directly into the room, bypassing the mediums. Some were reported to have wholly or partially materialized their bodies. Others could transport (or "apport," in the French-influenced lexicon of mediumship) a variety of physical objects into the room, apparently from distant locations in space and time.

Twice a week for five years, the Scole Group convened in their cellar, entered into a meditative state, and met with their Spirit Team for a total of about five hundred sessions. Because the Spirit Team insisted on an experimental environment as free of electromagnetic influences as possible, the below-ground cellar was an ideal venue, providing a good measure of radio silence. During the experimental sessions virtually all natural and artificial light was excluded at the request of the Spirit Team, who claimed that light of any kind—even infrared—would introduce an energy factor that would hamper their efforts.

Given these limitations it was essential to preclude the possibility of deception. So dim luminous adhesive tabs were applied to all movable objects in the room. The central table was designed to make any surreptitious manipulation impossible, and it, too, was fitted with luminous tabs. All participants wore luminous wristbands, so their hand movements could be monitored at all times. The bands were secured by Velcro strips, so any attempt to remove them would be instantly audible in the quiet cellar. Further controls included bolting the only access door from the inside during all sessions.

No electronic equipment of any kind was permitted by the Spirit Team, with the exception of two small audio cassette recorders. A consumer-grade unit was used as an experimental device, while a professional machine with a sensitive microphone documented every session in its entirety. From time to time still and video cameras were permitted, but for strictly limited use in particular experiments. The Spirit Team also advised the participants on the design of specialized equipment to enhance communication between their realm and ours.

How Was the Scole Experiment Monitored?

For a period of two years the Scole Experiment was closely monitored by three experienced and properly skeptical investigators from the London-based Society for Psychical Research (SPR): Professor David Fontana was a research psychologist and author. Montague Keen was a scholarly researcher and a historian of paranormal phenomena. Arthur Ellison was professor emeritus of electrical engineering at the City College of London. Here's what Fontana and Keen had to say about the experiment:

Skeptics are often unaware of the amount of experience and knowledge that goes into investigations of this kind. Between the three investigators you could say we've had fifty years and more of experience. . . . We know all the tricks!

PROF. DAVID FONTANA,
SPR INVESTIGATOR

At first we were pretty skeptical, because what had been reported was so way-out.

MONTAGUE KEEN,
SPR INVESTIGATOR

Over the experiment's five-year lifespan, sessions were conducted in the presence of hundreds of visitors, including scientists, engineers, and lawyers, as well as ordinary people from every walk of life. Other professionals included James Webster, a veteran stage magician and member of the UK's renowned Magic Circle society, who noted:

I could see no magic props or anything which made me feel inclined to think there was any hoaxing or trickery. I could not do it myself as a professional magician, and I don't believe that any magician that I knew could do even the [light effects] let alone the other phenomena that I witnessed.

Eventually sessions were conducted in the Netherlands, Germany, Switzerland, Spain, and the United States. Though some have speculated on how a few of the Scole phenomena *might* have been faked, at no time was any actual evidence of fraud or trickery detected by anyone.

What Phenomena Did the Scole Experiment Produce?

The full sweep of the phenomena produced at Scole goes far beyond the scope of this brief chapter. But as a photographer I think this is one of my personal favorites: In one session the Spirit Team reportedly asked the Scole Group to place a conventional camera, loaded with 35-millimeter color film, on the table in their darkened room. Soon the camera was heard to levitate and circle around the room, its shutter repeatedly clicking. The camera then settled back on the table. When the color film was developed, eleven perfectly framed black-and-white images appeared in both portrait and landscape formats. According to the Spirit Team, all were copies of photographs that actually existed somewhere in the world. This, they claimed, was undertaken as a first step because it was "easier than creating original images from scratch." Later the Group was asked to place fresh, sealed rolls of film directly on the table, without a camera. When developed, these displayed an astonishing variety of original imagery that often ran continuously along the entire length of the film, including the likenesses and signatures of notable deceased individuals, original artwork, whimsical puzzles, and even a signed, handwritten poem by the noted British poet William Wordsworth (1770–1850).

This led to a series of experiments using a VHS videotape camera, which yielded dozens of sophisticated, colorful, abstract, and semi-abstract images on *individual* video frames, as well as moving images of fluid light phenomena and animated faces. In some of these sessions the blank tapes used were selected, signed, and handled by Hans Schaer, a Swiss businessman and attorney, who personally attested to their genuineness.

Below are a few quotes from Scole participants about the materializations that took place during the experiment:

I really do feel that my Dad came, and he was the one who put his hands on my shoulders. . . . My chair was right up against a wall, and there was no way a person could be behind me.

ANDREA TUTONE, PHOTOGRAPHER
AND SCOLE VISITOR

Sometimes we would be touched by these hands. Sometimes we would invite them to touch us. . . . It felt like a normal human hand, and it grasped my hand firmly.

DAVID FONTANA,
SPR INVESTIGATOR

I felt an arm right in front of me . . . and I was so startled. I moved my hand up the sleeve . . . right up to the shoulder. And then it stopped. There was nothing beyond where the shoulder would have been. It was really an amazing experience.

PATRICIA LOAR, SCOLE VISITOR

According to the Scole Group, the Spirit Team explained that they usually materialized a hand or an arm because it was far easier than materializing a full body. But in some cases, even that was reportedly achieved:

I had the presence, the physical presence, of my mother, my father, and my sister, all in solid forms, standing in front of me. All of whom I was able to hold, to embrace, and to carry out conversations with them. I witnessed it so many times . . . it just becomes a normal thing.

ROBIN FOY, PRINCIPAL
SCOLE EXPERIMENTER

The physical objects that were apported into the room during the Scole Experiment apparently materialized out of thin air, and then fell, with a loud thud, onto the central table. Many were small objects—coins, jewelry, and such. But none were more exceptional or evidential than several British newspapers that arrived in pristine condition despite having been published during the war years of the early 1940s. These were analyzed by the Paper Industry Research Association and confirmed as genuine on the basis of their chemical composition, which was unique to that era. I held these papers in my hands about five years after they had arrived. Their outer pages had begun to yellow, but I can vouch for the fact that the inner ones remained as white as when they had come off the press, nearly sixty years earlier.

> *When a second-rate scientist says that this could not possibly happen, and many do, in connection with the paranormal, they are saying, in effect, that our current set of scientific models are the last word. And it would be ridiculous to say that. Scientific theories—descriptions—change all the time, and we must expect that to continue.*
>
> ARTHUR ELLISON, ELECTRICAL ENGINEER
> AND SPR INVESTIGATOR

> *I don't see how it could be faked. It's impossible.*
> J. CYNTHIA BROOKS, SCOLE VISITOR

Chapter 7 Summary

- The Scole Experiment took place in the small, historic English town of Scole, located in the county of Norfolk.
- The experiment comprised five hundred sessions conducted over a period of five years in the late 1990s.
- An unprecedented amount of physical evidence of paranormal origin was produced.
- Sessions were carefully monitored for two years by a team of skeptical investigators and witnessed by hundreds of guests, including scientists and engineers.
- At no time was any evidence of fraud or trickery detected.
- For much more information than I could squeeze into this chapter, check out *The Scole Experiment,* by Grant and Jane Solomon. *The Scole Report,* the complete scientific report issued by the Society for Psychical Research, is also available. *Witnessing the Impossible* is based on Robin Foy's extensive notes and audiotapes of the experiment's five hundred sessions.

• The story of the Scole Experiment is encapsulated in the eighty-minute feature documentary *Scole: The Afterlife Experiment,* coproduced by Tim Coleman and myself. The film features interviews with the Scole Group and its investigators and witnesses, reenactments of the Scole sessions, numerous excerpts from the actual Scole audio, video and photographic materials, and much more. You can see it at bit.ly/scolemovie.

8

The James Leininger
Reincarnation Case

James Leininger's story is one of the most touching, intriguing, and convincing reincarnation cases of modern times. James's detailed memories of a previous life and his parents' commitment to carefully researching and documenting them also place it among the most robustly supported reincarnation cases on record. If you haven't read about his story or seen it featured on TV, here's a very brief outline of the case and some links to more comprehensive information.

James was born on April 10, 1998, in San Mateo, California, to Bruce Leininger, a human-resources executive, and Andrea Leininger, a writer and former professional dancer. Shortly thereafter, the family moved to Dallas, Texas, and then to Lafayette, Louisiana.

As a toddler, James experienced frequent, uncontrollable nightmares and compulsively drew pictures of air battles. Confused and skeptical at first, his parents eventually came to terms with young James's obsession. When James's father took him to a flight museum at the age of two he correctly identified a particular World War II fighter plane, the Corsair, claimed to have flown one, and proceeded to point out some of its unique features and shortcomings.

Young James also recalled the name of an aircraft carrier: *Natoma*.

After searching the navy's online archives, James's father discovered that the USS *Natoma Bay* had been deployed in the Sea of Japan in March of 1945. Further research turned up references to a James McReady Huston Jr., a twenty-one-year-old pilot from Pennsylvania stationed on that carrier who had been the only American pilot shot down in a particular battle near Iwo Jima.

Young James Leininger recalled the name of another pilot in his squadron, Jack Larsen, whom James's father was eventually able to track down. Larsen turned out to have witnessed Huston's last moments as Huston's aircraft, which had been struck in its engine, plunged, ablaze, into the sea.

James's mother searched through census records and eventually tracked down and contacted Huston's surviving sister, Anne Barron, who provided a photograph of Huston and confirmed additional details of his life. She also confirmed young James's recollections about family names, nicknames, and relative ages, and that their father had been alcoholic.

When young James was brought to a reunion of the surviving *Natoma Bay* pilots, he recognized many of them—one by his voice alone. James said he also felt sad because "everyone looked so old."

James also reported between-lives memories. One of these concerned his having chosen his parents. Another included correct information about the period of time preceding his conception, including verifiable details of a Hawaiian hotel where his parents had been staying during a vacation.

James owned three G.I. Joe dolls, which he named Billy, Walter, and Leon. When his mother asked why, he explained "Because that's who met me when I got to heaven." James's parents later learned that three of Huston's squadron mates who had been killed prior to his own death were Billie Peeler, Walter Devlin, and Leon Conner.

These are but a scant few of the remarkable details of James Leininger's story.* The most comprehensive account of his case can be found in the best-selling book *Soul Survivor,* written by his parents with Ken Gross.

> *Awareness of cases such as James's—ones with documentation of a close agreement between events from a life in the past and memories a current child expresses—may lead the parents to be less likely to discount their children's reports and more able to help them through the experience.*
>
> JIM TUCKER, M.D.

Chapter 8 Summary

- As a young child, James Leininger was tormented by memories of having been shot down as a fighter pilot in World War II.
- James's recollections included numerous details of his former life and family, all of which were confirmed by subsequent research.
- James's story is perhaps the most thoroughly documented and widely reported reincarnation case of modern times.

---

*Other resources are numerous. In 2016 Jim Tucker, M.D., at the University of Virginia Health System's Division of Perceptual Studies, prepared a meticulously researched and documented report titled "The Case of James Leininger: An American Case of the Reincarnation Type." See also Jim Tucker's "Response to Sudduth's 'James Leininger Case Re-Examined.'" *The Psi Encyclopedia,* published by the Society for Psychical Research in London, includes an excellent article on the Leininger case. (The Greek letter Psi [Ψ] is often used as a symbol for parapsychology, psychical research, and psychic functioning in general.) The Reincarnation Research website offers a page titled "Soul Survivor: Past Life Story of World War II Fighter Pilot James Huston Jr./James Leininger." There are also numerous videos on YouTube that include, or feature, James Leininger's story.

PART III

The Nature of the Afterlife

Introduction to Part III

Imagine for a moment trying to describe and explain life on Earth to a fresh-faced alien newly arrived from Planet Zork. Obviously you can't cram something so infinitely complex into a nutshell. In any case, no two of us would describe Earth life to this hapless alien in quite the same way.

Describing and explaining what we call the afterlife isn't much different. Myriad attempts—scientific, metaphorical, fictional, poetic, scriptural, and autobiographical—fill countless volumes, ancient and modern. Go to Amazon's website, choose "Books," search on "afterlife," and over twenty thousand results come up. So in these chapters, I'll do my best to illuminate some of the most basic common denominators of the afterlife gleaned from a variety of private and published communications with those on the other side, as well as from firsthand accounts by near-death experiencers and those who claim to recall their life between lives.

Please keep in mind that our Western languages are built on the foundational assumption that the whole of reality is physical. So even our most specialized vocabularies can only hint at the nature and experience of a reality that appears to be larger than language. Esoteric texts, poetry, and so on may do a better job of it, but in the end words are only words, and each of us will respond to them in our own unique way.

As you read, please don't be too eager to reduce what follows to a single belief system or formula. A better approach might be to read between the lines and stay open to your own insight. See if you can let your framework of reality relax and expand a bit while staying focused on the main questions. Do your own research and seek beyond this book. Let your curiosity and understanding ripen and see where they take you. Please don't take anything that follows as the One True Account.

> *Belief is a form of self-protection. . . . When the mind is completely empty, only then is it capable of receiving the unknown.*
>
> J. KRISHNAMURTI,
> TWENTIETH-CENTURY SPIRITUAL TEACHER

9

What's It Made Of?

Arguably, the afterlife is made of the same great pool or ocean of energy that underlies physical matter. The difference is said to be mainly in the frequency range in which its underlying "substance" vibrates or oscillates, which is orders of magnitude higher than that of the relatively sluggish "building blocks" (particles and forces) that underlie the fabric of the physical universe.*

This pool of finer energies is said to be one and the same as consciousness itself. So we might say that the afterlife is literally made of the same consciousness that perceives and participates in it. How crazy is that? Perhaps no crazier than our body's being made out of the same substances that it perceives through its own physical senses.

Another difference is that, unlike the gross physical world of discrete objects, consciousness contains no fixed parameters, hard boundaries, borders, or limits as we normally think of them. To the extent that our language and concepts can describe it at all, it appears to operate "holographically" rather than spatially. In other words, every part of it may be in some sense distributed throughout the whole.

How crazy is that? Perhaps no crazier than our ability to dream, to understand, to hear our favorite piece of music in our minds, or to

---

*An excellent introduction to these "building blocks" can be found on YouTube in "A Video Tour of the Standard Model," *Quanta* (July 16, 2021). Recall also the explanation on page 19.

perceive the image of that elephant dancing in a pink tutu by simply imagining it.

> *I was told the garden was made of energy, not matter, and that I could touch it, but how it felt (rubbing the grass, for example) would be the way I expected it to feel.*
>
> JORDAN McKAY, AS CHANNELED BY
> HIS FATHER MATTHEW IN
> *THE LUMINOUS LANDSCAPE OF THE AFTERLIFE*

Chapter 9 Summary

- The afterlife, and everything and everyone in it, constitutes a sort of grand, oceanic hologram made of consciousness itself.

10
Where's It Located?

So where is this vast ocean of conscious energy—this "Greater Reality"—located? Experienced psychics, mediums, and intuitives* assert that it is not located in some far-off realm in the sky, but that we swim in it here and now. It extends infinitely but includes our universe, planet, country, town, neighborhood, home, and the immediate space around us and within our bodies.

But how could multiple frameworks of reality occupy the same space without interfering with each other? This isn't an especially radical notion. Think of the busy realm of radio and TV broadcasting and wireless communications, in which a multitude of channels (frequencies) pervade the entire extended space around us and even within us, silently and invisibly. They "don't exist" until we tune our receivers to resonate with the sources we choose. This automatically excludes, or filters out of our awareness, the ones in which we have no interest.

So how does tuning in and filtering out work? Here's a simple

---

*The difference between psychics/mediums/intuitives and the rest of us is that they appear to have the ability, through inborn talent, training, or both, to tune their awareness to what appear to be the higher frequencies of subtler realms. This opens up extended senses, known as clairvoyance, clairaudience, and clairsentience (clear psychic seeing, hearing, and feeling), and the ability to connect with minds that inhabit more rarefied levels of reality.

example: Imagine that you are completely deaf, but that you can tune in to a piano's heavy bass notes by putting your hands directly on the instrument and feeling its vibrations. The higher notes, however, would "not exist" for you, because their more delicate vibrations would be blocked or filtered out by the piano's heavy, solid mass as well as your own hands' limited sensory range. So music in any meaningful sense would be beyond your grasp. (And if you also happened to be a deaf pseudoskeptic, surely you would pounce harshly upon any nonsensical claims of "higher frequencies"!)

In this analogy, liberating our consciousness by whatever means (including leaving our dense physical bodies) would correspond to regaining our full spectrum of hearing and becoming directly aware of the whole range of the piano's musical vibrations.

Another analogy: Imagine that you had been blind from birth, so all the information that reaches normally sighted eyes had been excluded or "filtered out" of your awareness. At best you'd be able to discern only the general outlines, textures, and locations of nearby objects by touch, sound, or heat. But if your sight were then suddenly restored, your entire sense of reality would expand into dimensions of light, color, space, and form that had surrounded you all along but to all intents and purposes "had not existed," apart from the testimony of sighted individuals.

In fact, on the rare occasion that sight is suddenly enabled by surgery or other means, those blind from birth may need considerable time and training to adapt to a whole new sense of external reality—one that can be astonishingly different from what they might have previously imagined. This would be analogous to the experience of entering into the afterlife and having to acclimate to conditions there. We'll say more about this in the chapters that follow.

In dreams we already accept quite unusual representations of reality without a second thought. This suggests some of the ways in which a congenitally blind person might have a radically different inner picture of spatial reality than we normally perceive.* It also raises the question of how differently any two *sighted* individuals might actually perceive and make sense of their surroundings. Recall the discussion on so-called objectivity in chapter 5, and also consider the well-documented phenomenon of "synesthesia," in which an individual may smell colors, hear flavors, and so forth. So do we know with any certainty that what we might experience as a color isn't experienced as a flavor by others? Likewise, can we say exactly how any one individual might experience conditions in their afterlife? I don't think so.

> *[In the afterlife] the whole isn't located at a certain spot; it is located where you put your attention.*
>
> JORDAN MCKAY, AS CHANNELED BY
> HIS FATHER MATTHEW IN
> *THE LUMINOUS LANDSCAPE OF THE AFTERLIFE*

Chapter 10 Summary

- The afterlife is not located in some far-off "heaven," but can be thought of as a higher-frequency realm that interpenetrates, and coexists with, our familiar physical reality.

---

*Some years ago I lived in a rooming house in the Earl's Court district of London. On the floor above me three young women shared a flat. On asking one of the women about their roommate, I learned that the woman in question had been blind from birth, and that her father, an eye surgeon, had developed a procedure that eventually gave her sight. When they removed the bandages the first thing she saw was her father's face. This was such a profound shock that she required intensive psychiatric care until she could properly integrate her perceptions and come to terms with the utter strangeness of her new world.

11

How Does It Work?

First of all, what happens when we die?

Death is a transition.

FRANCES VAUGHAN, PH.D.

When you die, you take everything with you but the body.

RAM DASS

One thing that happens when we "transition" is that our bodily senses, which have connected us to the sluggish vibrations of the physical environment, are stripped away and the "veil" is lifted. So we may at first find ourselves feeling as if released from bondage, free to roam and explore limitlessly.

Some, however, may find themselves rather at sea, confused and disoriented as their interior reality has, in effect, become "externalized." In other words, the unconscious thoughts, beliefs, prejudices, and undealt-with emotions that they've carried with them in their psyche have "minds of their own" and can create unfamiliar virtual realities. These can range from ecstatic to upsetting; the latter can often manifest when one's death has been sudden or traumatic or there has been insufficient opportunity to prepare for it.

This isn't much different from how thoughts and emotions influence our experiences while we're embodied. In fact, it appears to be a continuation of the everyday psychological processes that take place in our waking lives and in our dreams, of which we're not consciously aware. But in the afterlife, without the stabilizing and grounding influences of the physical body and its environment, thoughts and feelings—conscious or unconscious—can "get real" very quickly.

Deeply ingrained expectations based on cultural or religious traditions can also impose their own illusory forms and images on our initial experiences of the afterlife.

Other deeply embedded emotions and beliefs can even cause some souls to get wholly or partly "stuck" between the worlds. This means that some of their psychological bits and pieces—say, their unloved child, jilted lover, or angry critic—may remain obsessively attached to the dissatisfactions of a real or imagined past in the physical world. In that case they may be unable to let go and pass over completely. This can give rise to endlessly recycled illusions and even "hellish" experiences in what is sometimes known as the "lower astral plane," or the "bardo realms." In extreme cases it may even manifest as the stubborn haunting of physical locations.

Fortunately, skilled healers and mediums from earthside can sometimes talk these hapless souls out of their trance and nudge them over the threshold. Or a guide or helper on the other side may reach out with love and reassurance and can entice them fully into the afterlife. Then, once the soul has all its pieces in harmony and unity, and its emotional issues adequately sorted out, it will be ready to move on.

Then what?

Once our soul has gathered all of itself up on the other side, one of the first things we learn is how to become increasingly aware of how our thoughts and emotions create what we take to be reality. Then we can begin to master these instead of letting them toss us about willy-nilly. With our faculties balanced and poised we can join the ranks of those who create and maintain "paradise islands in the Ocean of Consciousness"—distinct spheres of coherent reality in which all participants exist in an integrated state and experience loving, creative interactions and relationships. More about this below.

Mobility and Creativity in the Afterlife

If the "Greater Reality" of consciousness can be thought of as an infinite ocean, our souls might be likened to waves created, sustained, and animated by an unfathomable source of dynamic, vibrating energy. These soul-waves embody endless variety—no two are exactly alike.

Despite this infinite variety, the notion that our souls are all cut from the same cloth of consciousness implies that our fundamental relationship to each other—our starting point or default condition—is one of profound love and unity.

But to the extent that our souls are imbued with free will, we can springboard off that unity and in doing so create distinct "islands of reality" woven of focused thought patterns and stabilized by the magnetic force of shared imagery and meaning.

We do this by means of individual or collective intention, i.e., clear thoughts or visualizations of desired outcomes, which cause the "stuff" of consciousness to coalesce accordingly and take on corresponding forms. Investing sustained attention into these forms infuses them with coherence and endurance. This, we're told, is how "thoughts become things" in the afterlife. Calling on our earthside experiences and memories, we can re-create enduring facsimiles of familiar environments, from landscapes to cities. We can even mentally build and inhabit our own custom-designed dwelling places on individual or collective "reality islands."

When we do this individually, the result tends to be an insular, perhaps dreamlike, reality. When done in concert with other souls, the outcome is more like a stable creation of like minds. A living consensus reality.

We navigate and propel ourselves within the "space" of the afterlife by a similar process. Actively picturing a known destination sets us in motion toward it at a leisurely or rapid pace, or even instantaneously, depending on how intensely we desire to get there.

If these processes sound familiar it's because they parallel how we manifest our intentions and move about in the everyday physical world. After all, everything that exists in our human-made environment began with a vision, intention, or design, and every journey begins with a purpose or destination. While physical creativity may be slower and more cumbersome than it is in the afterlife, the general idea is very much the same.*

A Word about "Soul Orientation"— What It Is and How It Works

One of the Catch-22's of infinite soul variety is that not all souls may be equally capable of taking ownership of, or responsibility for, their actions and creations. For some, responsibility comes easily and can support their growth and evolvement. For others it may require herculean efforts, but these souls manage, and over lifetimes they learn and their evolvement accelerates. To whatever extent they take increasing responsibility, they can "keep their vibes up" and be "in service to the whole." In certain metaphysical traditions† this more evolved orientation is known simply as "STO"—Service to Others. Its outcomes tend to be life-giving, loving, creative, synergistic, and possessed of lightness and humor.

---

*In our physical lives, our actions and motions may be motivated by attraction, repulsion, or reaction. It's been said, however, that in the afterlife attraction is the main impetus to motion or action. This echoes the notion that in the afterlife one doesn't react against, or fight, negativity but instead endeavors to liberate souls who may be caught in it and who seek release. So rather than fighting fire with fire one extinguishes fire by simply removing its fuel. In our own world, an example of this principle might include the growing trend toward restorative, rather than punitive, justice. As Gandhi said, "An eye for an eye makes the whole world blind."

†See *The Law of One,* also known as *The Ra Material.* See also the website Operation Terra. (These mentions do not necessarily imply a blanket endorsement of either source.)

Souls that are unprepared to take responsibility (sometimes called "young" souls) tend to yield to unconscious thoughts and emotions associated with blind desire and blind fear. These give rise to shallow, coercive, and ultimately painful behaviors and relationships. This orientation is sometimes known as "STS"—Service to Self—and souls operating under this way of being tend to build "fortified islands in the Ocean of Consciousness." Since the inner resources of a young soul are weak and fragmented, it must put on shows of outward strength and take what it can get from others by whatever means.

Up to a certain balance point, negative STS behavior can play a catalytic role in the scheme of things by providing challenges that help keep STO souls alert and on their toes. It can motivate them to develop qualities and talents such as courage, patience, conscious loyalty, endurance, and the keys to creative problem-solving, which in a too-perfect world would otherwise lie dormant and undeveloped.

> It's the job of young souls to create karma.
>
> JANE KIMBROUGH

Beyond that balance point, STS behaviors tend to drain energy, waste resources, squander creative potential, and give rise to destruction and suffering. Does that sound familiar?

Fortunately in the afterlife like attracts like, and souls of a feather tend to flock together on their respective "islands of reality." These may represent commonalities of culture, belief, activity, and so forth, both positive and negative. Some souls, known as "wanderers" or "explorers," may journey among these realms to acquire a variety of experience and broaden their horizons.

Excursions by positive souls into deeply negative territory are normally conducted on a voluntary basis as "rescue missions." When new arrivals in the afterlife get stuck in uncomfortable spaces and call for help, these "first responders" can brave virtual fog, flood, and fire to snatch these hapless newcomers from the jaws of suffering and confusion.

My name is Mitchell, . . . I work with newcomers and was
here when you came into view. I shall take you, with your
permission, to a kind of sanatorium where I work. . . .
There they will go on helping you and giving you the right
conditions for health.

"MITCHELL," A RESCUER AND COUNSELOR,
TO A DISORIENTED T. E. LAWRENCE FOLLOWING
LAWRENCE'S SUDDEN DEATH, AS CHANNELED
BY JANE SHERWOOD IN *POST-MORTEM JOURNAL*

Chapter 11 Summary

- The process of creation in the afterlife hinges on intention and attention.
- Like minds tend to create consensus realities.
- When we pass over and leave our physical bodies behind, repressed or unconscious thought patterns and their accompanying energies can rise to the surface of our awareness and be projected as seemingly objective circumstances. These can be overcome with the aid of helpers and our willingness to see our "demons" for what they are.
- Souls may be more or less mature (consciously responsible for their creations). This variety and contrast keeps the pot of creation boiling, but beyond a certain point less-mature behavior can be destructive and wasteful. In the afterlife, just as in the physical world, it creates zones of individual and collective disharmony, from which confused souls may require rescue.

12

What's It Like?

So you've taken your last breath and the cord is cut. Now what?

As with our physical lives, each of which is unique, the best answer might be: it depends. Apart from certain commonalities, which we'll get to later, our experience of entering and abiding in the next world appears to be a highly individual matter, providing endless varieties of experience.

For example, if you're like Kalpana Chawla, the Indian-born mission specialist aboard the ill-fated space shuttle *Columbia,* you'll slip effortlessly out of your body, help your traumatized crewmates vacate their own fatally injured bodies, and move off into a realm that reflects your culture's most lovely and elegant creative and spiritual traditions. You'll visit your family back in India, who will be aware of your presence. Then you will reunite with your crew and help them heal and acclimate to their new home in the limitless nonphysical reaches of the cosmos. Later you'll relate your journey to mediums Jeanne Love and Regina Ochoa, who provide a transcript of the interaction at the Challenger Crew Channeling website.*

If you're like Colonel Thomas Edward Lawrence (a.k.a. Lawrence of Arabia), after racing over a hill, swerving to avoid some children on

---

*At the Challenger Crew Channeling website, click "Columbia" followed by "Text of Recordings."

bicycles, and wrecking your motorcycle, you'll leave your body, remain unconscious for a spell, and then awaken in a depressingly bleak landscape. You'll ask for help. Help will arrive, and you'll be taken to a supportive healing community. After a few years of Earth time, you'll dictate a remarkable book, *Post-Mortem Journal,* about your afterlife experiences through British medium Jane Sherwood.

If you're like Jessica, a young, tragically alcoholic hiker of my acquaintance who drowned in her bathtub, you might find yourself in a beautifully restorative environment with skilled healers, counselors, and picturesque hiking trails. Within a year you'll communicate with your parents and friends through a professional medium* who conveys your unique personal mannerisms and attitude with stunning accuracy.

If you're like my late partner Jane, who died after a five-year struggle with leukemia, you might find your soul visiting Florence, Italy— the one place on Earth you wanted to experience before you died but couldn't manage it—and then crossing completely to the other side and settling into a peaceful rural environment with your beloved, long-departed dog, Daphne. Over the course of a decade or more you'll manifest physical phenomena and communicate through four mediums as you evolve through various stages of your journey.

If you're like my intrepid sailor friend David, who chose Death with Dignity (medical aid in dying†) after a long, difficult illness, you might find yourself aboard your very own tall ship sailing over the bounding main of consciousness toward the vast horizon of an endless ocean.

If you're like my nerdy friend Neil, you'll have your body frozen and will hang around the cryo-preservation facility for months, desperately attached to that old body, until a friendly medium gently

---

*This and most other accounts in this chapter were shared privately by personal communication and are not available publicly, except as noted.

†For information on medical aid in dying, see the website Compassion & Choices.

points out that you could have much more fun and progress more rapidly in your evolvement by letting go and getting on with the rest of your afterlife.

If you're like Irina, a retired Silicon Valley scientist who took her life by leaping in front of a truck one night on Highway 101 in San Jose, California, you'll wallow for some time in regrets about how your act impacted the lives of the truck driver and the witnesses who happened to be driving by at the time. You'll then take time to heal, communicate through a medium of your acquaintance, and go on to work behind the scenes assisting and mentoring others in their scientific and spiritual work.

If you're like Frances Vaughan, a prominent transpersonal psychologist and author who died suddenly while out to dinner with friends, you'll connect psychically with Cynthia Spring, a still-embodied friend of yours. Together you'll write and publish a series of books about the Greater Reality and the urgency of our embracing it at this critical time in our history (*Seven Questions about Life after Life, Seven Questions about the Greater Reality,* and *Seven Stories to Light the Way Home*).

If you're like Jordan McKay, who was mugged and murdered one night in San Francisco at the age of twenty-three, you'll welcome your father Matthew's learning to channel via automatic writing so you can dictate *Seeking Jordan, The Luminous Landscape of the Afterlife,* and *Love in the Time of Impermanence,* which describe the nature of the afterlife as you experience it.

So What Are the Commonalities?

As the above vignettes illustrate, transitioning from this world to the next, and our experiences once we get there, can be as highly individual as our incarnated experiences—infinite variations on a theme. But what's the theme? What are some of the common denominators of the afterlife experience?

As reported by near-death experiencers and those communicating from the other side, an afterlife, like a physical life, appears to proceed in a series of developmental stages. These may include (but aren't limited to) the following, more or less* in this order:

- Feeling complete relief of physical pain and suffering, followed by the releasing of one's physical body—often called "cutting the cord."
- Hopefully letting go of any ego fixations or materialistic attachments, which, at this critical juncture, can tend to lock one (such as my nerdy friend Neil) into an obsessive identification with earthly forms.
- Habituating oneself to bodiless existence as a "point of perception." This includes 360-degree vision, "inner" hearing, and the absence of any weight, mass, or inertia. Strangely, this "point" remains linked to one's identity and its memories, including multiple lifetimes.
- Experiencing reality as "cleaner," "more real," and "less filtered" than it seemed during one's grossly embodied life.
- Mentally projecting a virtual body that is usually modeled after one's most recent incarnation at the prime of life. In this way one can interact in a more familiar and comfortable way with others, who themselves may project a prime-of-life image, or perhaps one of greater age or maturity, as they prefer. (These are not spatial projections as we might imagine them but more like imagery in a holographic matrix that appears in the inner eye of the beholder.)
- Being guided through a soothing virtual environment—often modeled after a beautiful natural landscape, garden, or a scene reminiscent of one's culture of origin.
- Learning and mastering the skills of personal mobility and creativity in a nonphysical environment, primarily *intention* and *attention*.

---

*Some of these stages may overlap, since in the Greater Reality physical time no longer rules and one may even enjoy simultaneous, parallel experiences. (If that sounds odd, just move your right forefinger in circles while moving your left in straight lines. See? Simultaneous experiences! Not so odd, is it? Now, extrapolate that to more complex possibilities . . .)

It's like learning to coordinate the knobs on an Etch-A-Sketch. One knob is your attention, and one knob is intention. If all you turn is the attention knob, you'll see whatever you think about. The intention knob is what you want to see or create.

JORDAN MCKAY, AS CHANNELED BY
HIS FATHER MATTHEW IN
THE LUMINOUS LANDSCAPE OF THE AFTERLIFE

Chapter 12 Summary

- As with our physical lives, everyone's afterlife experience is unique but based on certain underlying commonalities.
- Acclimating to the afterlife involves adapting to a different mode of existence. It entails learning new mental and emotional skills, with emphasis on *attention* and *intention*.

13
What's It For?

Thanks to the creative freedom available in the afterlife we might think of it as an "all-purpose" mode of existence. But here are some commonly reported options and opportunities:

- Meeting one's spiritual "pit crew"—guides, counselors, teachers, helpers and "angels," some of whom may at first strategically masquerade as trusted individuals or respected religious figures. These may include individuals who have paid their experiential dues as incarnate beings, as well as some who have never incarnated.

- Visiting still-incarnate friends and loved ones, who might at times be aware of one's subtle presence. Depending on one's energies, skills, and sense of humor, one may even signal one's presence by pulling pranks, such as switching lights or electronic devices on and off. In addition to being a gift of personal reassurance and assuaging grief, these phenomena can provide the sort of objective evidence that can help rational minds remain rational when considering the existence of an afterlife.

- Settling into a calm, supportive virtual environment that provides a stable base of operations for one's further healing, integration, and growth. This may mimic a familiar physical environment, such as a former home or favored spot. This environment will tend to be somewhat idealized, with no day/night or seasonal cycles unless desired.

▸ Reviewing the life just lived. This includes experiencing one's actions as others experienced them (Ouch!); appreciating the growth and wisdom one achieved; acknowledging all the good one brought into the physical world; and finally releasing negative emotional patterns and letting them unwind into calm, clean, neutral energy. This process may be relatively brief or extended. It may also include remembering one's past lives and ironing out problematic habits that have been repeated over the long arc of one's incarnations.*

▸ Attending classes led by advanced teachers.

▸ Being able, within limits, to perceive future events on Earth by sensing general patterns, trends, and probable outcomes. (Some have termed this the "balcony view" of earthly affairs.)†

▸ Communicating with loved ones, writers, healers, researchers, and ITC practitioners through mental and physical mediumship and interacting with physical communications technologies.

▸ Exploring the farther reaches of conscious emotion, including musical and artistic creation in dimensions of experience that are normally inaccessible to embodied souls.

▸ Exploring relationship, including experiences analogous to earthly collaboration, partnership, and even sexuality (either mimicking the

---

*The flamboyant mid-twentieth-century pianist Liberace, speaking through medium Jeanne Love, has described how he designed his life and lifestyle to compensate for a series of former lives of "piousness, poverty and suffering." The Cosmic Voices Network website has a transcript of his message. If you've never seen Liberace perform, check out "Liberace Mack the Knife" on YouTube (posted by Biggest Liberace Fan on May 12, 2016) to see an essential part of his message in action.

†Communicating the particulars of future events to those still incarnate tends to be strictly limited, partly because free will can change the trajectories of things already in motion, and partly to avoid overly influencing earthly affairs, which could give rise to unpredictable or counterproductive results. This parallels the notion of the "prime directive" popularized in the *Star Trek* TV series, which forbids meddling overtly in the affairs of developing civilizations.

physical experience or, at a subtler level, a sort of mutually transparent energetic merging).

▸ Participating in excursions that provide a "tourist's view" of Earth and other planetary systems and civilizations.

▸ Exploring the greater expanses of the physical and nonphysical universe, learning their underlying mathematics and structural and energetic patterns, and exploring the infinite variety of life forms native to Earth and other planets and life systems.

▸ Reuniting with one's "soul group" or "group soul"—a higher-level community entity in which each individual soul participates and shares the experience and wisdom it has gathered in its most recent incarnation. (A group member who is currently incarnate remains "present and accounted for" as the fraction of their being that always remains in the Greater Reality, because that connected fraction is the actual seat and source of an incarnated individual's consciousness.*)

▸ Deciding whether to reincarnate, and if so, where and when. (There are said to be many realms, physical planets, timeframes, adventures, and challenges to choose from.) With the guidance and support of loving, experienced guides and counselors, one chooses which path to pursue to reap the experiences that will best feed the evolution of one's soul. One hopes that this choice will ultimately contribute to the sum total of love, joy, and wisdom on our own planet, in the universe at large, and beyond.

▸ For those who have evolved as far as possible through the worlds of form, taking leave of form altogether and exploring realms beyond any finite description.

---

*As an analogy, think of using a search engine online: the search process takes place in the Greater Reality of the internet, not in our local physical devices, however sophisticated our devices might be. An even simpler analogy might be an electrical appliance plugged into a wall outlet: its actual power comes not from within its own physical embodiment, but from an invisible, distant source of potent energy.

▸ For those who have evolved as far as possible through realms beyond any finite description, merging with the Ocean of Consciousness, bearing the gift of one's accumulated learning, wisdom, and love.

I no longer view ordinary reality as the only reality. There's a whole other reality, and that reality is the bigger one. This one is just a transitory experience; you're only here for a certain number of years, but the other one is infinite . . . it's ineffable ecstasy and union . . . This material world is basically just a short pit stop.

MICHAEL HARNER,
ANTHROPOLOGIST

Birth is not a beginning, death is not an end. There is existence without limit; there is continuity without a starting point.

CHUANG TZU,
TAOIST PHILOSOPHER, 300 BCE

It might turn out to be that the human species is much more a nonphysical than a physical one.

WHITLEY STRIEBER, AUTHOR

You are as dead now as you will ever be.

SETH, A NONPHYSICAL TEACHER POPULAR
IN THE LATE TWENTIETH CENTURY

Wow! Oh, wow!

THE FINAL WORDS OF STEVE JOBS,
COFOUNDER OF APPLE

Chapter 13 Summary

- The afterlife, like physical life, tends to progress in broad developmental stages that can be rich, varied, and unique to the experiencer.
- Eventually one's cycle of soul development is fulfilled and one is absorbed into the wholeness of consciousness.

Epilogue

What Do We Know, and Where Do We Go from Here?

If the evidence offered in this book is valid, the existence of a Greater Reality—a matrix in which our awareness and sense of self apparently dwell between our physical lives and in which our entire physical universe may itself be embedded—appears to be beyond question.

The fact that this matrix exists beyond the reach of our narrow senses, our current scientific instruments, and our language does not rule it out. Meanwhile, mounting positive evidence for its existence rattles the gates—and gatekeepers—of our academic, scientific, and cultural institutions.

Breakthroughs are being made in psychic and electronic communication with the "other side." Stringent academic research is being conducted into reincarnation, mediumship, terminal ludicity, and other previously neglected fields of inquiry. Newly developed or rediscovered techniques and practices are building bridges between this world and the next. All these and more are inexorably forcing the question of an afterlife into the light of day, following centuries of passive neglect and active avoidance or suppression by our dominant academic, scientific, and religious institutions.

This book is only one small contribution to the emerging flood of science-based afterlife-related litereature. Turn to the resource section and recommended reading list for several suggestions—the most important being to read as widely as you can and see which perspectives mean the most to you.

And if you are so inclined, gently broach the subject to others. You may be surprised at how many will welcome sharing their own thoughts and experiences relating to the afterlife.

I hope this rising tide of awareness maintains its momentum toward a courageous, responsible approach to answering the eternal questions surrounding the deeper experience and meaning of life and death.

All goes onward and outward, nothing collapses,
And to die is different from what anyone supposed,
and luckier.

WALT WHITMAN

Resources

The Conference on Death, Grief and Belief (formerly called the Afterlife Awareness Conference)
The conference brings together scientists, researchers, hospice professionals, spiritual teachers, and grief counselors to share their knowledge about end-of-life care, near-death experience, and after-death communication, as well as conscious dying and conscious grieving.

Afterlife Research and Education Institute (AREI)
The AREI supports afterlife research and education and explores our nature, as Pierre Teilhard de Chardin put it, as "spiritual beings having a physical experience."

The Big Circle
On this website/blog, the parents of young people who passed before their time have posted EVP recordings of their children and others who communicate from the other side. (To access this site, search "welcome to eternity.")

The Challenger Crew Channeling
This website is affiliated with the Silicon-Valley-based Foundation for Mind-Being Research. It features transcripts of voluminous channeling sessions that began in 1986 when mediums Jeanne Love and Regina

Ochoa were apparently first contacted by the crew of the ill-fated space shuttle *Challenger*. More recently the crewmembers of the shuttle *Columbia,* which was destroyed on reentry in 2003, have apparently come through with extensive contacts. These are available on this site as audio recordings and transcripts.

Cosmic Voices Network
This site is a collaboration of mediums Jeanne Love and Regina Ochoa, psychic/author Cynthia Spring, and myself as webmaster. It features transcripts of channeled messages from a long and growing list of individuals, both well known and obscure, who have been eager to share their afterlife experiences with those of us still in the body.

Forever Family Foundation
The foundation's focus includes support and healing for the grieving, and furthering afterlife science through research and education.

The Foundation for Mind-Being Research (FMBR)
The FMBR's mission is to expand the context of scientific exploration to include both its physical and nonphysical aspects and to create partnerships that foster innovative solutions for the challenges facing our world today.

The Institute of Noetic Sciences (IONS)
The institute's mission is "to reveal the interconnected nature of reality through scientific exploration and personal discovery." IONS is a research center and laboratory specializing in the intersection of science and human experience.

International Association for Near-Death Studies (IANDS)
IANDS's purpose is to promote responsible, multidisciplinary exploration of near-death and similar experiences, their effects on people's lives, and their implications for beliefs about life, death, and human purpose.

The Scientific and Medical Network
A leading international forum for people engaged in creating a new worldview for the twenty-first century.

University of Virginia Department of Perceptual Studies (DOPS)
Founded in 1967 by Dr. Ian Stevenson, the Division of Perceptual Studies is a university-based research group devoted to the investigation of phenomena that challenge mainstream scientific paradigms regarding the nature of the mind/brain relationship. Researchers at DOPS are particularly interested in studying phenomena related to consciousness functioning beyond the confines of the physical body, as well as phenomena that suggest continuation of consciousness after physical death.

The Windbridge Research Center
The center's mission is to ease suffering around dying, death, and what comes next through rigorous scientific research, the results of which are shared with the general public, clinicians, scientists, philosophers, and practitioners, including mediums.

Relevant Documentaries
Calling Earth. 2018. Directed by Daniel Drasin and Tim Coleman. bit.ly/callearth or https://vimeo.com/101171248
Scole: The Afterlife Experiment. 2009. Directed by Tim Coleman and Daniel Drasin. bit.ly/scolemovie or https://vimeo.com/573225843

Recommended Reading

Books

Alexander, Eben. *Proof of Heaven.* New York: Simon and Schuster, 2012.

Assante, Julia. *The Last Frontier.* Novato, Calif.: New World Library, 2012.

Benedict, Mellon-Thomas. *Journey through the Light and Back.* Naples, Fla.: Purple Haze Press, 2019.

Blumenthal, Ralph. *The Believer.* Albuquerque, N.Mex.: High Road Books, 2021.

Buhlman, William. *Adventures Beyond the Body.* San Francisco, Calif.: HarperSanFrancisco, 1996.

Cardoso, Anabela. *Electronic Contact with the Dead.* Hove, UK: White Crow Books, 2017.

———. *Electronic Voices: Contact with Another Dimension?* Winchester, UK: O Books, 2010.

———. *Glimpses of Another World: Impressions and Reflections of an EVP Operator.* Hove, UK: White Crow Books, 2021.

Dunne, J. W. *An Experiment with Time.* Charlottesville, Va.: Hampton Roads Publishing Co, Inc., 2001 (First published in 1927).

Eisenbud, Jule, M.D. *The World of Ted Serios, Second Edition.* Hove, UK: White Crow Books, 2021.

Fontana, David. *Is There an Afterlife?: A Comprehensive Overview of the Evidence.* Ropley, UK: O Books, 2005.

Foy, Robin. *Witnessing the Impossible.* Diss, UK: Torcal Publications, 2008.

Hopkins, Lloyd F. *Training Manual for Sight Without Eyes—Through Mind Sight and Perception*. Seattle: Clear Springs Press, 2008.

Kastrup, Bernardo. *Why Materialism Is Baloney: How true skeptics know there is no death and fathom answers to life, the universe, and everything*. Alresford, UK: Iff Books, 2017.

Keen, Montague, Arthur Ellison, and Fontana, David. *The Scole Report*. London: Society for Psychical Research, 2011.

Kübler-Ross, Elisabeth. *On Death and Dying*. New York: Scribner, (1969) 1997.

Leininger, Bruce, Andrea Leininger, and Ken Gross. *Soul Survivor: The Reincarnation of a World War II Fighter Pilot*. New York: Grand Central Publishing, 2009.

Macy, Mark. *Miracles in the Storm: Talking to the Other Side with the New Technology of Spiritual Contact*. New York: New American Library, 2001.

McKay, Matthew. *Love in the Time of Impermanence*. Rochester, Vt.: Park Street Press, 2022.

———. *The Luminous Landscape of the Afterlife*. Rochester, Vt.: Park Street Press, 2021.

———. *Seeking Jordan: How I Learned the Truth about Death and the Invisible Universe*. Novato, Calif.: New World Library, 2016.

McNamara, Sean. *Mind Sight: Training to See Without Eyes—Pilot Program for Adults*. Denver, Colo.: Mind Possible, 2021.

Monroe, Robert. *Journeys Out of the Body*. New York: Broadway Books, 1971.

———. *Far Journeys*. New York: Broadway Books, 1985.

———. *Ultimate Journey*. New York: Broadway Books, 1994.

Moody, Raymond. *Life After Life*. New York: Harper Collins, 1975.

Moorjani, Anita. *Dying to Be Me: My Journey from Cancer, to Near Death, to True Healing*. Carlsbad, Calif.: Hay House, Inc., 2012.

Newton, Michael. *Journey of Souls: Case Studies of Life Between Lives, Fifth Revised Edition*. Woodbury, Minn.: Llewellyn Publications, 2019.

———. *Destiny of Souls: New Case Studies of Life Between Lives*. Woodbury, Minn.: Llewellyn Publications, 2010.

Ring, Kenneth. *Life at Death*. New York: William Morrow & Co., 1982.

———. *Heading Toward Omega*. New York: Harper Perennial, 1985.

———. *The Omega Project*. Fort Mill, S.C.: Quill House, 1993.

Ring, Kenneth and Sharon Cooper. *Mindsight: Near-Death and Out-of-Body Experiences in the Blind*. Palo Alto, Calif.: The William James Center for Consciousness Studies at the Institute of Transpersonal Psychology, 1999.

Ring, Kenneth and Evelyn Elsaesser Valarino. *Lessons from the Light: What We Can Learn from the Near-Death Experence.* Needham, Mass.: Moment Point Press, 2006.

Roberts, Jane. *The Afterdeath Journal of an American Philosopher; The World View of William James.* Port Washington, N.Y.: New Awareness Network, 2001.

Sherwood, Jane. *Post-Mortem Journal: Communications from T. E. Lawrence.* London: Neville Spearman, 1964.

———. *The Country Beyond.* Saffron Walden, UK: C.W. Daniel Co., Ltd. 1991.

Solomon, Grant and Jane Solomon. *The Scole Experiment (Updated Edition).* Waltham Abbey, UK: Campion Books, 2006.

Spring, Cynthia and Frances Vaughan. *Seven Questions about Life after Life.* El Cerrito, Calif.: Wisdom Circles Publishing, 2019.

———. *Seven Questions about the Greater Reality.* El Cerrito, Calif.: Wisdom Circles Publishing, 2020.

———. *Seven Stories to Light the Way Home.* El Cerrito, Calif.: Wisdom Circles Publishing, 2022.

Sheldrake, Rupert. *Dogs That Know When Their Owners Are Coming Home.* New York: Three Rivers Press, 2011.

Strieber, Whitley and Anne Strieber. *The Afterlife Revolution.* San Antonio, Tex.: Walker & Collier, Inc., 2017.

Van Lommel, Pim. *Consciousness Beyond Life: The Science of the Near-Death Experience.* San Francisco, Calif.: HarperOne, 2011.

Waggoner, Robert. *Lucid Dreaming: Gateway to the Inner Self.* Needham, Mass.: Moment Point Press, 2008.

Waggoner, Robert and Caroline McCready. *Lucid Dreaming, Plain and Simple.* San Francisco, Calif.: Conari Press, 2015.

Yong, Ed. *An Immense World: How Animal Senses Reveal the Hidden Realms Around Us.* New York: Random House, 2022.

Scientific Articles

Bastos, Marco Aurélio Vinhosa Jr., et al. "Frontal Electroencephalographic (EEG) Activity and Mediumship: A Comparative Study between Spiritist Mediums and Controls." *Archives of Clinical Psychiatry* 43 no. 2 (March–April 2016).

Braude, S. E. "Mediumship and Multiple Personality." *Journal for the Society of Psychical Research* 55 no. 813 (1988): 177–95.

Bem, Daryl, et al. "Feeling the Future: A Meta-Analysis of 90 Experiments on the Anomalous Anticipation of Random Future Events." US National Library of Medicine, National Institute of Health (January 29, 2016 version).

Carhart-Harris, Robin L., et al. "Neural Correlates of the LSD Experience Revealed by Multimodal Neuroimaging." *Proceedings of the National Academy of Sciences* 113, no. 17 (April 11, 2016).

Costandi, Mo. "Psychedelic Chemical Subdues Brain Activity." *Nature* (January 23, 2012).

Delorme, Arnaud. "Electrocortical Activity Associated with Subjective Communication with the Deceased." *Frontiers in Psychology* 4 (2013): 834.

Else, Holly and Richard Van Noorden. "The Fight Against Fake-Paper Factories That Churn Out Sham Science." *Nature* (March 23, 2021).

Hageman, Joan J., et al. "The Neurobiology of Trance and Mediumship in Brazil." *Mysterious Minds: The Neurobiology of Psychics, Mediums and other Extraordinary People* (January 2010): 85–111.

Halberstadt, Adam and Mark Geyer. "Do Psychedelics Expand the Mind by Reducing Brain Activity?" *Scientific American* (May 15, 2012).

Kean, Leslie. *Surviving Death: A Journalist Investigates Evidence for an Afterlife.* New York: Crown Archetype, 2017.

Kluft, Richard. "Commentary on 'Multiple Personality and Channeling.'" *Jefferson Journal of Psychiatry* 9, no. 2 article 13 (1991).

Shared Crossing Research Initiative. "Shared Death Experiences: A Little-Known Type of End-of-Life Phenomena Reported by Caregivers and Loved Ones." *American Journal of Hospice and Palliative Care* 38, no. 12 (April 5, 2021): 1479–87.

Tucker, Jim. "Response to Sudduth's 'James Leininger Case Re-Examined.'" *Journal of Scientific Exploration* 36, no. 1 (Spring 2022).

Wahbeh, Helané, et al. "Exceptional Experiences Reported by Scientists and Engineers." *Explore* 14, no. 5 (September 2018): 329–41.

Index